Living F.I.T

A 40-DAY GUIDE TO *Living* Faithfully, Intentionally, and Tenaciously

Gabriella Marigold Lindsay

Requests for information should be addressed to:

Email: gabriellamlindsay@gmail.com

First Printing, 2016

ISBN-10: 0-692-75559-4
ISBN-13: 978-0-692-75559-4

Cover Design and Interior Layout: Forerunners Ink LLC

Printed in the United States of America

DAY BY DAY

ACKNOWLEDGMENTS

Thank you first and foremost to God for enabling the writing of this book. Thank you to my husband, Vernon, and our three children—Vizuri, Emery, and Mkazo—for your support and enthusiasm throughout this process. Finally, thank you to the myriad people who have inspired, encouraged, educated, and supported me and this work. You are all appreciated and admired more than you know!

PREFACE
Success Leaves Clues: A Handy Coach's Guide

Below are some helpful tools to use when planning your day. I recommend using the Nutrient Timing as discussed on Day 10 as a means to help optimize your metabolic rate. Plug your wake-up time into the sample below and space remaining meals with a window of 2.5 to 4 hours between each. Leave at least two hours (but no more than three hours) between your last meal or snack and bedtime.

Sample Nutrient Timing
6:00 A.M. – Healthy Breakfast
9:00 A.M. – Protein-Rich Snack One
12:30 P.M. – Healthy Lunch
3:30 P.M. – Protein-Rich Snack Two
7:00 P.M. – Healthy Dinner
9:30 P.M. – Bedtime

*Optional Snack Three – (no closer than two hours before bedtime)

Here are some of my favorite breakfast, lunch, and snack combinations. Mix and match to find your ideal menu! I place the bulk of my carbohydrates and fat in the morning hours of the day, which gives me the energy (and time) I need to utilize them most effectively. I aim to keep my dinner and my optional third snack lower in carbohydrates as my body is typically less active during this time.

Healthy Breakfast Suggestions (high protein, moderate carbohydrate, low-moderate fat)

- Egg white omelet with fresh veggies
- Steel cut overnight oats (made with low-fat milk or soy milk)
- Ezekiel toast with nut butter and turkey sausage or turkey bacon
- Egg white mini-muffins
- Meal replacement shake or protein enhanced fruit and veggie smoothie

Protein-Rich Snack Suggestions (high protein, moderate carbohydrate, low fat)

- Apple or pear, 12 almonds (raw, unsalted), wheat crackers
- Hard boiled eggs (2), half grapefruit
- Greek yogurt (fat-free) parfait with granola, nuts, berries
- Cottage cheese (fat-free) and peach or plum
- Bell pepper strips and hummus with wheat crackers
- Celery or carrot sticks with 2 tbsp of nut butter
- Scrambled egg whites and Ezekiel toast slice

Healthy Lunch Suggestions (high protein, moderate carbohydrate, moderate fat)

- 4-6oz Chicken breast, ½ cup brown rice, 1 cup green beans
- 4-6oz Seafood (shrimp, crab, scallops, etc.), ½ cup quinoa, 1 cup broccoli
- 4-6oz Tilapia, ½ cup couscous, 1 cup cabbage
- Extra lean ground turkey burger, 1 wheat sandwich thin, lettuce, mustard, onion, tomato
- 4oz Tofu, 1 cup mixed veggies, ½ cup whole grain noodles

Healthy Dinner Suggestions (high protein, low carbohydrate, low fat)

- 4-6oz Chicken breast atop green leafy veggies with fresh raw veggies and 2 tbsp low-fat dressing
- 5oz Tuna (in water) tossed with parboiled veggies (broccoli, carrots, cauliflower) and 2 tbsp low-fat dressing
- 4oz Extra lean ground turkey, ¼ tomato sauce, 1 cup spaghetti squash
- 4-6oz Tilapia, 10 spears of asparagus
- 4-6oz Seafood (shrimp, crab, scallops, etc.) sautéed with 1 tbsp olive oil, spices, atop spiralized zucchini squash
- 4-5oz lean steak, ½ sweet potato (plain), 1 cup green veggies

INTRODUCTION
A Note on How to Use Living F.I.T.

First and foremost, I would like to thank you for choosing this book. I am excited to spend the next forty days with you on this amazing journey. During the course of this program, it is my sincerest hope that you will be inspired and encouraged to live your life faithfully, intentionally, and tenaciously. This book is designed to help you develop a routine for living a healthy, active, faith-based lifestyle that brings you much happiness and fulfillment.

How to get the most out of this book

I recommend beginning Day 1 on a Monday. Mondays are good for various reasons. For most people, Mondays signify the beginning of a new week and a familiar routine. By beginning on a Monday, you will have the opportunity to do any grocery shopping or meal preparation before starting the program in earnest.

There are two types of daily entries for you to read. The devotional entries begin with a guiding Scripture, continue with words of Scripture-based encouragement and a prayer, and close with an actionable step to take. The health-based entries begin with a wellness lesson, continue with a prayer, and conclude with an action instruction. These entries alternate day by day. I recommend reading each entry as a part of your early morning routine so that you are equipped with new knowledge and can carry your **F.I.T.** tip with you into your day.

Before beginning, please take a look at the **Handy Coach's Guide** in the preface for suggestions regarding daily food and water intake, timing of meals, snacks, fitness, and more. I encourage you to also invest in a fitness and meal tracker to assist you with accurate calculation of your caloric intake and output.

In the appendix, you will find a variety of recipes that I use in my own kitchen. They are tasty, easy to make, use very few processed ingredients, and are nutritious. Some are original recipes, while others are old family favorites made with a healthy twist. Feel free to use any or all of the recipes as a part of your daily meal preparation. I also recommend using the Internet to uncover other recipes or the Simple Swaps guidelines (page 55) to help create your own new favorites!

My hope is that you will find the information and guidance within these pages useful during these forty days and beyond. Living a healthy, active, faith-based lifestyle is a lifelong process. These forty days are just the beginning of the creation of something wonderful and life-changing. Congratulations on taking your first step toward living **F.I.T.**

Of course, before beginning this or any form of physical or nutritional health program, consult with a doctor regarding any current health concerns or recommendations.

DAY 1

Just Begin

And do not be conformed to this world, but be transformed by the renewing of your mind, that you may prove what is that good and acceptable and perfect will of God.
Romans 12:2

There is no right time. There is no Monday or January 1st. Just begin. Today. *Now!* Far too often, we find ourselves talking ourselves out of something. "I'm not ready," "I'm not good enough yet," "Maybe after X, Y or Z happens first." Does that sound like you? I know I have fallen victim to it many times—even in the writing of this book! I found myself, like you, struggling to find the "right time" and discovering, in reality, all I was doing was setting up roadblocks and using delay tactics.

When it comes to implementing a new habit, and particularly a healthy, active, faith-based lifestyle, I encourage you just to begin. Take a small step today—right now—in the right direction. Drink a glass of water, drive past your favorite fast food restaurant without stopping, get out of the house and walk to the end of the block or skip the elevator and head for the stairs. You don't have to be perfect to start, but you do have to start to see progress. Renew your mind, ask God to show you what is in His will for your life, and move into action.

God desires continual transformation. He desires that you grow spiritually and physically. Do something today to take even the smallest step in that direction. Begin by refreshing your awareness and being good to your body. Your body is a vessel from which to perform God's work. Treat it with respect and kindness, and Lord willing, it will provide you with many beautiful earthly years to come.

What is holding you back from beginning? How can the renewal of your mind-set make a change in your life? What small step can you take today to just begin?

Gracious God, thank you for showing me an opportunity to begin a new journey. Thank you for the encouragement and strength to start making changes in my life. In Jesus' holy name, amen.

F.I.T. Step

In what way does your mind-set need to change in order to create a new lifestyle for yourself? Make a list of three (or more) thoughts that have held you back in the past and commit to breaking past those barriers.

DAY 2

The Benefits of Healthy Eating

Long before we became a fast-food nation, our ancestors were hunter-gatherers. They lived off of the earth they roamed, relying on meats and berries, fruits, vegetables, and grains. Foods were whole and hearty, satisfying and fortifying. Today's foods are mere remnants of that. They are processed, grown with hormones and antibiotics, and preserved to last months, even years, on warm grocery store shelves. Today's people have turned to immediate gratification and the lure of more-bang-for-your-buck size upgrades.

While many Americans claim to know that eating healthy is good for them, it is important that we explore the benefits of healthy eating here, as this is critical to understand during this journey. Healthy eating can:

- Help you maintain a healthy weight
- Help you fight off illness and disease
- Increase your energy levels and increase mental clarity and alertness
- Save you money in health care and associated costs
- Contribute to maintaining manageable food budgets, especially for large households

Knowing this, we can choose to use food as our best medicine, not our quickest poison. We get the opportunity to choose foods that will fuel our minds and bodies and enhance our lived experience. Through the course of this program, we will uncover the secrets of making healthy eating easy and enjoyable. We will discuss ways to create a lifestyle based around healthy eating and active living so that it becomes something natural and fun. The power to make a change is in God's will, and it is through faith-based mindfulness that you can make a change and be empowered to eat healthily and live healthy every day!

Awesome God, thank you for providing for my needs. Please show me how eating healthier can help me live according to your will. I desire to be healthy and happy should you see fit. In Jesus' holy name, amen.

F.I.T. Step

It's cleaning time! Go through your pantry, refrigerator, and freezer and donate or dispose of foods that will derail your results. Examples include potato chips, cookies, ice cream, soda pop, and candy.

DAY 3

Your Why

The Lord will guide you continually, and satisfy your soul in drought, and strengthen your bones; You shall be like a watered garden, and like a spring of water, whose waters do not fail.
Isaiah 58:11

My kids are my *why*. Most everything I do revolves around them, including practicing healthy habits. Not only do I want to live a long, happy, active life with them, but I also want to set a good example for them so that they too can be healthy. What brought you to this point? Was it a health scare? Are you unhappy with what you see in the mirror? Do you want to be more active with your children? Do you simply want to get your "swag" back? No one reason is better or worse than any other, and no one reason has been statistically proven to produce greater or longer-lasting results than another. It isn't the reason that defines the outcome; it is the depth and clarity of your purpose that shapes the result.

What is your why? Why have you decided to make a change? Meditate on that. What makes your why so important to you? Focus on your why and visualize how being in better health will impact it. Does it mean more years with your loved ones? Does it mean fewer doctor's visits? Does it mean more energy to do the things you love with the people who matter most? Perhaps it means more time on earth to do God's work!

God wants us to be healthy. God desires for us to be an ever-flowing stream, a well-watered garden, so that we may be of service to others according to His will. God will guide us and provide for our lives. As God's vessels, we have the unique opportunity to bless His name by striving to stay in good health and of sound body and mind. Your why is intertwined with God's direction for your life. Trust in Him, believe in your God-given abilities, remember your why, and continue moving forward, towards good health and renewed vitality.

Most gracious God, thank you for this day. Please allow my why to be stronger than my why not. Continue to guide me and allow me to be healthy and vibrant like an ever-flowing stream. In Jesus' holy name, amen.

F.I.T. Step

Write down your goal and your why. Speak your goal and your reason aloud. You can speak this to a friend or partner or aloud to God in privacy. Speaking the words aloud will bring power and life to your intention.

DAY 4

What Is Healthy Eating?

We have talked about some of the benefits of healthy eating, but what exactly is healthy eating? Healthy eating comprises a few components:

- **Whole foods** - food that has been subjected to little (or no) processing or refining and is free from additives, preservatives, or other artificial substances. Examples of whole foods include whole fruits and vegetables; basic grains such as brown rice, quinoa, and whole wheat flour; fresh meats; and natural dairy.
- **Water** – important for healthy body function, digestion, the elimination of toxins. Aim to drink half your body weight in water ounces each day. Reduce reliance on sugary juices, sodas, and alcoholic beverages.
- **Portion Control** – your eyes are bigger than your stomach. Stick to fist-sized portions of lean meats, thumb-sized portions of fats, palm-sized portions of grains, and load your plate up with green veggies such as steamed broccoli, fresh spinach, cabbage, or kale.
- **Balanced Meals** – consist of a complex carbohydrate, a lean protein, and a vegetable. Having, at minimum, three balanced meals each day is critical to maintaining good health, an active metabolism, and helps

ensure the consumption of the proper vitamins and minerals.

Are you currently eating healthy meals made up of whole foods? Is your diet 80 percent or more "clean"? Meaning, are the majority of your meals being prepared at home in a healthy manner from minimally processed foods? Do you find yourself frequently driving through fast food lanes and grabbing packaged snacks from vending machines? How about water? Do you drink large amounts of juice or soda? Over the next forty days, I challenge you to reduce your consumption of processed, fast, convenience foods and to increase your water intake. These two steps, coupled with a moderate increase in physical activity, can result in better health, increased energy, and reduced weight.

Dear Lord, thank you for the resources to eat healthier. Please guide my hand while I shop and steer me away from old temptations. Please help me make good decisions that will better my health. In Jesus' holy name, amen.

F.I.T. Step

Plan a portion controlled, balanced meal for dinner tonight. Incorporate strategies from today's lesson in creating it. Use baking, broiling, roasting or steaming as cooking methods to keep food fresh tasting and lower in fat.

DAY 5

Your Past Is Not Your Present

Casting all your care upon Him, for he cares for you.
1 Peter 5:7

Worry, regret, anxiety, and frustration are all natural human emotions we experience regularly. Many times people struggle with decisions they have made in the past that they wish they could go back and correct. If only we had a *Back to the Future* style DeLorean and could travel through the space-time continuum to reverse some of the actions (or inactions) of the past. Well, we cannot—and actually, that's okay! God allows those things in our lives as learning opportunities. He does not want us to dwell in the past. Instead, He wants us to learn from those experiences and move on in a direction that is pleasing to Him.

Maybe a past decision creeps its little head up, and a wave of regret washes over you. Maybe it is a missed opportunity, a failed relationship, or even just a cruel word uttered in the heat of the moment that has made a significant impact on your life or the life of someone else. Maybe it is an addiction or compulsion that guided you into a dark place that haunts you still to this day. Cast those negative thoughts and feelings, that sadness and anxiety, on God. He will provide for you because He cares for you.

Today is the day to let it all go. Today is the day to cast

your worries on God and breathe in new life. Your past does not define who you are today. What has happened in days long gone has undoubtedly shaped who you are in the present, but it does not define you! Release those feelings of guilt, hurt, shame and defeat, and embrace the love and light that can be found in God! Each day you walk with God you are renewed. Let His healing presence rejuvenate your spirit, and allow His light to guide your path and order your steps. Learn from your mistakes, but do not allow them to shackle you in your present. Belief and trust in God will set you free from the pain of the past. God is on your side, and He will walk with you through your present.

Dear God, thank you for being an ever-present friend. I pray that you continue to care for me, love me, and guide me. Please strengthen me as I make changes in my present and release the pains of the past. In Jesus' holy name, amen.

F.I.T. Step

On a sheet of paper, write down the things that are holding you back. Then rip, flush, burn, or otherwise dispose of that paper and release the anxiety along with it. God is in control!

DAY 6

Breakfast:
The Most Important Meal of the Day

Missing shoes, spilled milk, dirty diapers, crabby spouses, and misplaced homework are just a few challenges many of us struggle with each morning as we attempt to get where we're going in a timely manner. Oftentimes, it is easier to overlook breakfast with plans to grab something en route or at the office when the time of departure is heavily looming. Unfortunately, this is a common mistake with substantial repercussions. Remember when your mother told you that breakfast was the most important meal of the day? She wasn't just telling you that because she really liked cereal. She was truly on to something!

Breakfast, literally, breaks the fast that your body has been in overnight. Without sustenance for upwards of twelve hours overnight, the body goes into fat storage mode. This means that the metabolism (that important little thing that helps us burn calories and use them for energy) has dropped significantly. In order to awaken the metabolism and jump-start the fat burning process, it is important to consume a high protein, moderate carbohydrate, low-fat meal within 30-60 minutes of awaking. Once your body is in fat-burning mode, not only will you see increased weight loss results over time, but you will also feel more energized and alert throughout your day.

I never miss breakfast. I love breakfast. Like really, really,

really love breakfast! My breakfast usually consists of a protein rich meal replacement shake, but on occasion I opt for a healthy power-packed combination such as an egg white scramble, turkey sausage, and whole grain toast or a piece of fruit. There are many combinations of healthy breakfast food options you can try. It does not need to be complicated! The easier, the better and the more likely you are to stick with it. So, if fruit and granola-topped yogurt sounds like paradise or a convenient on-the-go protein shake or bar is more your speed, take the time to prepare something for yourself and enjoy. The people you encounter will appreciate your calmer, more energized and alert demeanor, and your waistline will thank you too!

Heavenly Father, thank you for blessing me with the opportunity to have a healthy meal each morning. Please equip me with the discipline needed to create a healthy breakfast habit. In Jesus' holy name, amen.

F.I.T. Step

Set your alarm right now to give yourself an additional fifteen minutes for tomorrow morning. Remind yourself before going to bed tonight that tomorrow you will make time for a healthy breakfast before rushing out the door.

DAY 7

Living Faithfully

Therefore I say to you, whatever things you ask when you pray, believe that you receive them, and you will have them.
Mark 11:24

Faithfulness comes in many shapes and sizes. You can be faithful to a spouse or significant other, promising never to seek comfort in the arms of another. You can be faithful to your job, arriving punctually and giving your best effort every day. You can be faithful to your health by eating right and exercising regularly. God also asks us to be faithful to Him: to rely on Him to help us through the dark times and to thank Him for His gifts along the way. Are you living faithfully? Are you relying on God to bring you through your darkest moments and having faith that even in those moments, God's got it?

For me, it has been my faith in God that has gotten me through my struggles. I have faith that even moments of turmoil have been placed in my path as a reminder that God is truly in control and that I must rely on Him to guide me through. Maybe you too have experienced moments of hardship when it is hard to see through to the other side. Maybe you have questioned why God has forgotten about you or why He has made things so troublesome. It's normal to have questions; yet God asks us to have faith and take heart that He is on our side. God answers prayer! He loves us unconditionally and never places anything in our lives that, with His grace, we cannot handle.

I remind myself daily to seek God. I encourage you to do the same. Seek God when you're cheerful and thank Him for the wondrous bounty He has bestowed upon you. Seek God when you're feeling low and ask Him for guidance and the fortitude to remain faithful to Him as He steers the course. Just as you remain faithful to the things you enjoy and the people you love, remain steadfast and faithful in your love for God and His Son, Jesus Christ. Pray for the ability to believe and be reinforced with His unwavering love every day. Living faithfully is freeing, and with the burden of worry placed in God's hands, you can move mountains!

Heavenly Father, thank you for the abundant blessings you have bestowed upon me. I pray that you hear the meditations of my heart and that they be in alignment with your will for my life. I pray for continued faithfulness and steadfastness. In Jesus' holy name, amen.

F.I.T. Step

Before beginning each day, take a moment to lay in bed and say to God, "I surrender control and I have faith in your will." Listen for His voice throughout the day and trust His guidance.

DAY 8

The Power of Protein

Protein is a powerful ally in the journey to a healthier you. It is essential for weight loss, the building of lean muscle, and the proper nourishment of vital organs. Folks who are able to maintain a healthy body weight are likely to have diets higher in protein than those who are at an overweight or obese body fat percentage. Why is that? Protein provides the following benefits to the body:

- It helps maintain body weight by making you feel fuller longer.
- It stabilizes blood sugar levels.
- It helps increase lean muscle mass (when combined with exercise).
- It improves mood and healthy brain function.
- It promotes heart health and longevity.

Many Americans enjoy carbohydrate-heavy meals such as heavy portions of pasta, fattening pizza, heaping piles of French fries, and oversized slices of cake. As a result, they do not get the daily recommended amount of lean protein in their diets. When your body is lacking in protein, you may notice the following symptoms:

- Trouble losing weight due in part to a sluggish metabolism.

- Low energy levels and fatigue.
- Poor concentration and trouble learning.
- Moodiness and muscle, bone, and joint pain.
- Blood sugar changes that can lead to diabetes.
- Slow wound healing and frequent colds.

So, how do you know if you're getting enough protein? There are many tools available on the Internet that will help you calculate your recommended protein intake based on your gender, height, weight, and fitness level. A general rule of thumb recommended by the DRI (Dietary Reference Intake) is 0.36g of protein per pound of body weight. An easy way to increase your protein intake is to commit to eating one lean protein option at every meal and snack. Boneless, skinless chicken breast, fish, seafood, lean and extra lean ground turkey, beef and chicken, tofu, low-fat and fat-free dairy (cheese, yogurt, milk, etc.), fat-free milk, soy milk, beans, low-sugar protein shakes and bars, and even small servings of nuts are all great ways to increase your protein intake!

Creator, thank you for this day. Please help me to transition my nutrition habits, dear Lord. I acknowledge the need for healthy lifestyle choices, and I look to you to support me in making the right decisions. In Jesus' holy name, amen.

F.I.T. Step

Incorporate one lean protein at every meal and snack today. Feel free to use any of the above options while planning your day. Continue to consume lean protein through the remainder of this program, and make it part of your daily nutrition routine.

DAY 9

On Comparison

For do I now persuade men, or God? Or do I seek to please men? For if I still pleased men, I would not be a bondservant of Christ.
Galatians 1:10

Facebook, Instagram, magazines, television shows—nearly everywhere we look, we see picture-perfect people. We see youthful couples living happy lives with amazing spouses, two-and-a-half kids, a dog, and a house with a white picket fence. We see gorgeous celebrities in tiny bikinis and powerful athletes in peak physical condition. Even in real life, it seems we all have that one friend who has it all together and, from our standpoint, is just really good at everything! The bombardment of our minds with perceived perfection can be overwhelming, and studies have shown it can lead to increased levels of depression and social seclusion. But why is this?

When we as Christians know that God is the only perfect one, why do we still cling to such idols and turn friends, family members, and even complete strangers into our gods? Comparison. It's human nature to compare. We are of the world and of the flesh, and it is within reason to begin to make comparisons between ourselves and others who may have the "stuff" we want for ourselves.

Galatians 1:10 warns us about this, which gives us pause

to reflect. Are we trying to win the approval of our peers or God? Certainly, I am striving to receive the approval of the Creator,;but then again I am human, right? And darn it, my neighbor's home is beautiful, her kids are always well behaved, and she looks super cute in her designer jeans. *Arghhhhh! What do I do?!*

It is a daily challenge for me to keep my eyes on God when it comes to the things of the world, but I am encouraged when I remind myself that only God is perfect, and that we all have our own personal struggles to overcome. His presence alone uplifts my spirit, pushes me to concern myself only with doing His work, and invigorates me to keep my eyes on Him. Keeping my eyes on Him and Him alone helps me to turn my moments of "Man, I wish I was like her" to "Gee, I'm proud of her accomplishments!"

President Theodore Roosevelt stated, "Comparison is the thief of joy." I pray that you will commit alongside with me to keeping your eyes on His perfect grace and to letting the things of the world that try to steal your joy fall by the wayside. Be an encourager and be encouraged that you need not compare yourself with others around you. Take note, it is wise to be the best you that you can be and work daily to please God with your body, mind, spirit, and works.

Heavenly Father, thank you for another day to sing your praises. Please help me to seek only your approval and not the approval of others. Please help me to stop comparing myself to others and to encourage others on their journey. In Jesus' holy name, amen.

F.I.T. Step

Throughout the remainder of the day, cut out any unnecessary social media usage. Take away the distractions that lead you to make comparisons. Refrain from comparing yourself to others and work toward pleasing God.

DAY 10

Nutrient Timing

For effective weight loss, it is essential that your body's metabolism be in optimum working order. Everyone's metabolism works differently, and some body types, environments, hormonal fluctuations, and lifestyle choices can cause metabolism to work slower than ideal. Barring any underlying medical issues, however, it is possible to boost metabolism naturally through nutrition and exercise! One way to boost the metabolism is by eating more. More? Yes, more!

Eating at regular intervals, about every three to four hours throughout the day, will help your body stay in fat-burning mode. When your body is in fat-burning mode, it is using the calories you're consuming most effectively, ultimately leading to faster weight loss. When the body is unsure of when its next meal will come, it will hold on to all of the food energy (read: fat and calories) rather than using it to fuel and energize you. This can lead to delayed weight loss and even weight gain!

An easy way to think about this is to relate it to bears in hibernation. Before hibernating, a bear will eat a large quantity of food. It is because the bear knows it will be without food for many days to come. The bear's body stores the fat, nutrients, and calories as energy to sustain him through many nights in the cave. Upon waking, however, the bear is back to his old tricks, looking for food to sustain his energy. We, like bears, also hoard fat and calories for energy when our bodies are unsure when our next meal is coming. To keep your metabolism in peak operating condition, I recommend training your body to anticipate sustenance by consistently eating smaller meals and snacks at regular intervals throughout the day to maintain a healthy metabolism and encourage healthy energy levels.

Dear Father, thank you for your guidance and for giving me the energy to continue. I pray that you show me how to make excellent decisions and help me stick to my nutrient timing. Please equip me with the tools needed to be successful today. In Jesus' holy name, amen.

F.I.T. Step

In order to be successful with nutrient timing, set an alarm on your phone to go off every three hours to remind you to stop what you're doing to have your meal or snack. Over time, your body will adjust, and you will find you do not even need the alarm to remember to eat. Your body will let you know!

DAY 11

Tuning Out the Noise

I waited patiently for the Lord; and He inclined to me, and heard my cry. He also brought me up out of a horrible pit, out of the miry clay, and set my feet upon a rock, and established my steps. He has put a new song in my mouth—Praise to our God; many will see it and fear, and will trust in the Lord..
Psalm 40:1-3

My home is very noisy. I have three kids aged five, four, and nearly three. I have a husband who plays musical instruments and "sings." If it's not the noise from the kids' toys or the televised sing-along, then it's the dishwasher, washing machine, or vacuum filling our space with sound. The noise in my house often makes client consults, writing, and even peaceful conversation difficult. I have to lock myself in a room or sometimes even hide in a closet simply to get some peace and quiet! While the noises of a happy household definitely bring me much joy, they are also a source of distraction that sometimes make projects take longer than I desire and cause me to make mistakes. As a result, I get the opportunity to work hard to tune out the noise.

What noises do you need to tune out? Is it noise in the literal sense: phones, social media, reality TV, and so on? Is it spiritual noise: doubt, depression, temptation? God can help you tune out any kind of noise you desire to release. He will help you to focus and complete tasks. He will help lift your mood, and He will remove enticement from your life. If you keep your ears and heart open to Him and His great Word, He will send you a message that will be timely and relevant.

God is waiting to help us. He is waiting for us to seek His wisdom and good counsel. If we wait patiently, He will hear our cry and put a joyful song in our mouths! How encouraging! How exciting! How comforting to hear that, despite the noise we are surrounded by, God can hear the needs of our heart and He indeed cares! Glory!

What noises will you ask God to help you tune out today? What concerns will you put in the Lord's hands? When you seek the Lord, He will come. Put your trust in Him, and He will give you much strength!

Dear God, thank you for another beautiful day designed by your hand. Please help me to tune out the noise in my life. Allow me to see and hear you more clearly. I ask you for guidance, for clarity, and for peace of mind. In Jesus' holy name, amen.

F.I.T. Step

Identify the noises that are in your life. Which noises are helpful and which noises are preventing you from focusing on the things that matter? If the noise can be set aside, do so! Release the things that are weighing you down and blocking you from your blessings.

DAY 12

The Importance of Hydration

The human body consists of a significant amount of water. In adult men, about 65 percent of the body is water and in adult women, about 55 percent of the body is water. Water is integral to keeping vital organs lubricated and healthy, and it is essential for healthy digestion, a major key to weight loss. As a rule of thumb, I advise my clients to drink half their body weight in fluid ounces each day, up to 128oz (one gallon). I recommend increasing that amount by 20 to 40 ounces if my clients have had an intense workout or when they've spent a good amount of time outside in the heat and sun.

While on this journey, I recommend that if you are not already drinking water, you should start. Begin by replacing sugary sodas and juices with drinking water, sparkling water, or even water infused with lemon, lime, or other tasty fruit ingredients if you need a little taste refresher. The benefits of drinking water are many. Here are a few:

- Water gives the body life-sustaining energy.
- Being properly hydrated can improve brain function.
- Drinking water can reduce the occurrence of migraines.
- Water can improve digestion and elimination.
- Increased water intake helps aid weight loss.

At the outset, drinking more water may seem difficult. You may find yourself running to the bathroom frequently. That is a good sign; it means you're flushing out toxins and fat! As your body becomes adjusted to the increased water intake you will find over time that you are not rushing to the bathroom with as much frequency. With increased water intake, be on the lookout also for clearer skin, increased energy and better digestion. Water is a truly amazing health partner!

Heavenly Creator, thank you for this day and for the abundance of fresh, clean water. I am aware that not everyone is blessed with clean running tap water, and I pray that it is in your will to see that all the world is blessed with the resources they need for good health. In Jesus' holy name, amen.

F.I.T. Step

Today, I encourage you to drink one full gallon of water. That is 128 ounces. Spread the water across the day, drinking sixteen ounces with each meal, eight ounces with each snack and sipping on water throughout the day. You may add lemon, lime, cucumber, or mint to liven up your glasses!

DAY 13

Intentional Living

You shall love the LORD your God with all your heart, with all your soul, and with all your strength.
Deuteronomy 6:5

When I held a full-time position as an assistant principal at an elementary school, something I learned from our school's principal was the importance of being intentional with your actions. Everything she did was purposeful. While not always apparent at the time, down the road it was obvious that a well-laid stone had been placed on a path toward something bigger and more important. Being in the presence of someone who lived her life with such intentionality was truly a blessing. I learned that while the destination is important, the journey towards that end is paramount.

Your car's GPS works in the same way. Before leaving point A, it has calculated the route to point B. Provided that there is no detour causing roadblocks, you will arrive (God willing), happy and whole and in a timely manner. Ah, but the roadblocks. The GPS was not anticipating those. Neither were you! But guess who knew about them? And guess who has a plan for you to get beyond them?

God is intentional. He has a plan for your life, and He will test your fortitude while strengthening and encouraging you.

I am excited to live an intentional life that begins with loving God first and foremost. Do you love God first? Do you thank Him for all the goodness He has given you? Do you live on purpose for His purpose?

The work we do here on Earth prepares us for our reconnection with God in heaven. By carrying out the deeds He has set forth for you here on Earth, you will be prepared to receive the joys and riches of heaven that await you. Are you living your life in the Word? Can others attest to the light of faithful intentionality that radiates through the words you speak and the actions you take? The enemy may throw a barrier in the road, but you must continue walking the path of intentionality. Indeed, if it is God ordained, each small step will bring you closer and closer to living a life built for God's glory.

Dear God, thank you again for your love and light. Please help me to live a life of intentionality and please bless the stones that are laid on my path to you. I desire a life lived for your glory. In Jesus' holy name, amen.

F.I.T. Step

What has God laid on your heart today? He has already ordered your steps for the day. Before making important decisions or significant choices today, be mindful and listen out for God's instruction. He will be your GPS, and He will not steer you wrong.

Day 14

Fail to Prepare, Prepare to Fail: Do Your Meal Prep

After many failed attempts, I discovered the only way I would be successful in reaching my health goals was to have a set plan and meals at hand. I am flawed. If I see something that looks tasty, and I am hungry, I will eat it. However, when I have prepared meals and snacks right at my fingertips, I am much less likely to make poor choices.

Here are some ways to make meal prep easy and, of course, check out the recipes in the appendix for some delicious meal ideas!

- **Buy in bulk.** Plan your meals for the entire week; make a list and spend one afternoon at the grocery store. Shopping just once a week will save time, money, and energy.
- **Keep it simple.** Choose one or two meals you will eat for breakfast, lunch, and dinner during the week. Create a daily meal plan. Keep meals simple and add variety by using an assortment of fresh herbs and spices.
- **Set aside time to cook.** I enjoy using early Sunday morning before church as a time to complete meal prep for my and my husband's breakfast, lunch, and snacks for the week. I have also carved out time during my week to prepare meals for our family dinners that work around our lives.

- **Use pre-portioned snacks or create your own.** You can purchase 100-calorie packs of your favorite snack foods like almonds, whole-wheat pretzels, and even Greek yogurt. You can even save money by buying full-size packaged goods and using zipper bags and reusable containers to create your own perfectly portioned to-go packs. Use the serving size on the package as a guide, pack them up for the week, then grab and go!
- **Be realistic.** Do you typically snack in the car? Maybe a yogurt parfait isn't for you. Choose meals and snacks that will easily complement your lifestyle. No microwave? No problem! Pack a lunch meat sandwich or crisp green salad.

While the thought of meal prep may seem daunting, over time you will find ways to make it fun and easy! Enlist the help of your household and make it a family affair. Once you've found recipes you enjoy, you will begin to memorize them and even add your own delicious embellishments. As you practice and experiment, the task of preparing your food will become enjoyable … and your health results will reflect your good efforts!

Heavenly Creator, thank you for your love. Please help me to exercise the discipline needed to prepare healthy meals for each day and to remain focused on my health. In Jesus' holy name, amen.

F.I.T. Step

Create a meal plan menu that you will use for five days. Commit to purchasing the ingredients, preparing and packaging the meals, and only eating what is in your plan for the day each day. No extra snacking or sampling!

DAY 15

There Is Strength in Numbers

Though one may be overpowered by another, two can withstand him. And a threefold cord is not quickly broken.
Ecclesiastes 4:12

I love being in large groups. Ever since I was a child, I have enjoyed being in group activities ranging from figure skating to academic study groups, Bible studies, and fitness classes. I love going on double dates with other couples, and I enjoy taking my kiddos out to the playground or meeting up with other moms for play dates. Maybe it's the only child in me, but there's something about having like-minded folks surrounding me and supporting me in whatever it is I am doing—that is just magical.

The Bible also tells us that having a partner or even a small group can be beneficial when the enemy comes and tries to take hold. There is a strength in numbers that will help ensure that you will not be defeated.

That translates easily to the healthy, active lifestyle journey you are on. There will come days when you are tempted to give up or to give in to temptation. Some days, making it to the gym just seems impossible. Other days, you may have a difficult time resisting the temptation of the freshly baked donut and sweet roll breakfast at your early morning meeting. Experiencing temptation is normal. What you do with the experience is what sets you up for success or disappointment and is reflective of your commitment to living a life for Christ. Remember, you are not in this alone. God is with you and will always be your number one cheerleader. Finding a family member or a like-minded friend from your church or office to pair up with can turn a good experience into an amazing journey. Become accountability partners and support one another during the tough times and celebrate one another through the "wins"! Having a support system can make all the difference in the world.

So reach out, share, ask (you might be surprised who says yes), and you will be amazed at how strong a force together you can be.

Dear Lord, thank you for this life. I pray that you direct me to people who will be open to joining me on this journey. I know I am capable, and I pray for the support of others. In Jesus' holy name, amen.

F.I.T. Step

Reach out to a friend at work who can become a fitness partner. Commit to meeting at a set time each day to walk the stairs of your building or take a brief walk during your lunch break. You can even find a partner at your children's school, the local park, or your gym.

DAY 16

Benefits of Exercise

Kids run everywhere. From the moment they learn to toddle around, they begin to run. Sometimes seemingly at the speed of light! As we age, however, many of us steadily start to slow down.

Sedentary desk jobs, long hours commuting to and from various destinations, cold weather, injuries, weight gain, and so on, all give us reason to slow down and become less active. However, remaining energetic in our adult years is critical to good health; and one way we do that is by exercising.

The benefits of exercise, much like the benefits of proper nutrition, are numerous. Let's explore!

Exercise:

- Keeps your body and brain fit and able.
- Improves sleeping patterns and reduces anxiety.
- Lowers high blood pressure, lowers the risk of diabetes, and improves cholesterol levels.
- Improves body image, eating habits, muscle strength, and joint function.
- Increases energy level, adds fun and happiness by reducing stress, and boosts mood.
- Enhances a weight loss regimen and improves overall quality of life.

There are many other reasons to exercise. What reason(s) resonated with you? Why are you excited to incorporate exercise into your daily lifestyle?

Dear God, thank you for the ability to use my body today. Please give me the discipline to exercise and the stamina to complete the activity. In Jesus' holy name, amen.

F.I.T. Step

Aim to exercise today for thirty minutes. You can select the type of activity: walking, jogging, elliptical, biking, hiking, climbing stairs, a group class, etc. It doesn't really matter what you do, but doing it with enthusiasm, 100 percent effort, and consistency is what will help create a new enjoyable habit.

DAY 17

The ABC Song

But seek first the kingdom of God and His righteousness, and all these things shall be added to you.
Matthew 6:33

One of my kids' favorite songs is the ABC Song. It's one of the first songs they learned and felt compelled to memorize. While they occasionally skip letters, as adults, we likely do it in our sleep with no problem. But here I ask you, do you know your ABCs?

Ask. Do you ask God for the things you desire? Do you ask God to guide you to help you to do His will? Do you ask God to consider the needs of friends, family, your church, and your world? Do you ask God to strengthen you in every walk of life? *Ask, and it will be given to you; seek, and you will find; knock, and it will be opened to you. Matthew 7:7*

It's simple enough really—if you ask God, He will answer and supply.

Believe. How will we receive the abundant blessings that God has for us if we do not believe? He cannot enrich our lives if we do not believe in His power and ability to do a work in us. Are you a believer? *The Lord is my strength and my shield;*

My heart trusted in Him, and I am helped; Therefore my heart greatly rejoices, and with my song I will praise Him. Psalm 28:7

Surely, we all have our moments when we have to dig into our faith. We might have to take a leap when we cannot see what God is doing behind the scenes. Do you have the wherewithal to withstand those tests and believe in Him?

Conceive. God will answer your questions, and He will bless your life abundantly, but you must do the work. This applies to everything, from building a relationship, to developing a business, completing a degree, or getting healthy and active. Without your fortitude and taking the intentional actions God is directing you toward, you will accomplish nothing. *And if you are Christ's, then you are Abraham's seed, and heirs according to the promise. Galatians 3:29*

Your blessings are there. They are your inheritance! God desires for you to be a diligent worker, someone who is willing to roll up his or her sleeves and go to battle for His good.

So now you know your ABCs, next time won't you Ask, Believe, and Conceive with me?

Heavenly Father, thank you for continually guiding me. Please continue to bless me with the ability to ask, believe, and conceive of the gifts you wish to place in my hands. I do all things for your glory. In Jesus' holy name, amen.

F.I.T. Step

Today is as good a day as any to begin walking the walk. Is there something God has placed on your heart to accomplish? Possibly you've heard the call to start a business or participate in a ministry at church or even reach out to a long-lost relative. Do it today … don't delay!

DAY 18

Complex Carbohydrates

Complex you say? What's complex about carbs? I see them; I eat them. Simple as that!

Carbohydrates get a bad rap. Everyone from television celebrities to medical doctors tote the benefits of no-carb and low-carb diets. Do they work? Certainly! When we deprive ourselves of any major food group and drastically reduce our caloric intake, significant weight loss will occur. But is it necessary to ban all carbohydrates and live off of lean protein and vegetables alone? No. Moreover, is doing so practical and sustainable over the long-term? Most emphatically, no! So, how can we have our proverbial cake and eat it too?

We can do so by choosing the best type of carbohydrates we can. We can choose whole, minimally processed, complex carbohydrates. Complex carbohydrates provide our bodies with the energy and fuel we need to sustain our day-to-day activities without the over-processed, excess sugar calories we do not need. Examples of complex carbohydrates include brown rice, whole-wheat pasta, couscous, quinoa, sprouted wheat bread, beans, whole fruits and vegetables, and oats. These complex carbohydrates are actually good for our bodies and can help us lose weight!

When used in moderation, these complex carbohydrates, made of long chains of sugar molecules that are absorbed quickly, provide long lasting energy and help maintain healthy body weight. Additionally, when selected in place of simple carbohydrates (the white processed stuff like white bread, white pasta, sugar, etc.), complex carbohydrates can actually encourage healthy weight loss! Many complex carbohydrates also contain the right amount of heart-healthy fiber, which encourages healthy elimination and promotes a feeling of fullness. So, there's no need to always pass the bread; simply choose the least processed, most natural whole grain bread possible and enjoy in moderation!

Dear God, thank you for giving me the knowledge to choose better. Please give me the strength to just say no to the things that will derail me from the results meant for me. In Jesus' holy name I pray, amen.

F.I.T. Step

Say no to anything "white" today. No white rice, white pasta, white flour (pancakes, waffles, bread, etc.), sugar, cereal (unless it's a whole grain/no sugar added variety), candies and pop. Consistently replace those foods with their complex carbohydrate counterpart and enjoy the increased energy, reduced cravings, clearer skin, and weight loss results you will see!

DAY 19

Walking in Your Greatness

Having then gifts differing according to the grace that is given to us, let us use them: if prophecy, let us prophesy in proportion to our faith.
Romans 12:6

There is a greatness inherent within you. That greatness comes from God. He has bestowed each of us with unique gifts and talents to be used for kingdom building here on earth. Isn't that amazing? I am excited about and proud of the gifts God has given me, and I am so blessed to share them! It hasn't always been this way, however. It has taken time, thought, and fervent prayer to discover that my gifts were meant to be shared, designed to be praised, and destined to change lives. Now, proclaiming your greatness may make you feel uncomfortable or even boastful. As a society, embracing and asserting your gifts can be misconstrued as being egotistical or prideful, but would God have given you those gifts if He didn't want you to use them? I think not.

My church firmly believes that "everyone is a ten in something." Maybe you're an engaging writer, a beautiful singer, a math whiz, or a restorative healer. Whatever it is you excel at, know that it is an amazing gift from God and that He wants you to use that gift for the good of others. We have been blessed with an incredible vessel here on earth and have been handed a bounty of gifts we are encouraged to use along our earthly walk. You are a ten in something! Embrace that and begin to walk in your greatness. God wouldn't want it any other way!

If you are unsure of your gifts, there are ways to discover them. Start with your passion. What excites you? Maybe you love to work in your garden in the morning, or maybe you enjoy caring for children. Others may find pleasure in physical activity while still others may find that reading, writing or tabulating statistics makes their pulse race. Can the things you enjoy doing be used to promote the Good News or spread the love of God to others? If so, that right there could be the gift God wants you to use for Kingdom building!

Whatever it is, God is telling you something, and He is telling you in a big way! Answer Him by embracing His call, praising His name, and proclaiming His gifts in your life. Take the reins, accept success and dare to walk boldly in your greatness!

Dear God, thank you for blessing me with many gifts. Please show me how to use my gifts to bless you and bring joy and your Word to others. In Jesus' holy name, amen.

F.I.T. Step

Make a list of the things you enjoy or are particularly gifted at. Can any of these tasks be used at your church or in your community? Consider using your God-given talent(s) today and in the future as a way to bless God through walking in your greatness.

DAY 20

Simple Swaps

Eating healthy does not have to be boring. Certainly, it should be something that can be enjoyed by the whole family! I have made it a point in my household to make our meals fun, tasty, and nutrient rich. Sometimes, making a simple swap can make a huge difference in weight loss and health results. Here are some favorite simple swaps my family loves:

- **Infused Water** – Instead of sugary lemonade or juice, use a variety of fruits like lemons and strawberries to create refreshing water that is low in calories and big on taste.
- **Stevia** – Replace traditional sugar in many baking recipes, as well as in protein smoothies, coffee, and tea with all natural, zero calorie stevia.
- **Greek Yogurt** – Choose nonfat Greek yogurt in recipes calling for sour cream. Fat-free Greek yogurt has a creamy, tangy taste; it boosts the protein and keeps fat and calories low.
- **Extra Virgin Olive Oil and Coconut Oil** – These oils can replace high cholesterol butter in recipes as both provide health benefits unparalleled by butter, while still delivering delicious flavor.
- **Low-fat and Fat-Free Dairy** – This is preferable because many low-fat dairy items like cheese, cottage

cheese, yogurt, etc., still taste great while reducing saturated fat and calories.

- **Extra Lean Ground Turkey** – Choose this in place of traditional ground turkey, ground chicken, and beef since it is equally delicious and lower in saturated fat.
- **Brown Rice/Whole Wheat Pasta** – Both are less processed, higher in protein, more nutrient dense, and more filling than their enriched, processed, traditional white counterparts.
- **Fresh/Frozen Vegetables** – When available, always use these instead of canned veggies, which are full of sodium and preservatives.

It is amazing what a few simple swaps can do to promote weight loss and a healthy lifestyle! Adding more nutrients, protein, and whole foods can significantly reduce cravings, clear the intestinal system and provide more energy naturally! The next time you visit your local grocery store, I encourage you to purchase a few of these simple swap items and see for yourself how small changes can produce delicious, healthy meals at affordable prices!

Heavenly Father, thank you for providing me with nutritious options every day. I ask for your help in finding and enjoying delicious and nutritious swaps that will help me reach my health goals. In Jesus' holy name, amen.

F.I.T. Step

Choose four of the above simple swaps to incorporate into your meal plan. Finding options that you like may take time, effort, and adjustment, but it will be well worth it!

DAY 21

A Lasting Impression

Now Jesus and His disciples went out to the towns of Caesarea Philippi; and on the road He asked His disciples, saying to them, "Who do men say that I am?"
Mark 8:27

You've probably heard the expression First impressions last a lifetime. Upon meeting someone new, you will remember if the person was confident or shy, kind or mean-spirited, genuine or distrustful. That first impression can shape how you view him or her, potentially for years to come. The first impression, however, does not have to be the final or lasting impression.

According to the Gospel of Mark, as Jesus traveled through new villages, there were those who thought him to be arrogant, lying and deceitful. By caring for the ill, weak, and troubled; performing innumerable miracles; and giving freely of himself, Jesus' actions turned many people's initial impressions around for the better!

We too can work to reverse people's initial impression of us. Are you that hard-hearted soul who is frowning or unhappy? Are you quick to judge others or point out mistakes? Are you quiet and meek, often yielding to the will of others? Are you pleased with the first impression you are giving? If you find yourself, like many others, struggling to express all the beauty and wonder that is inside of you, I advise you to seek God's help.

God gave Jesus the fortitude to press on despite how He was treated. God gave Jesus the sight to continue to believe regardless of what the naysayers said. God gave Jesus the power to heal, restore, and love others unconditionally. You are blessed with some of those same abilities! We can tell of God's love through words, but even more importantly we must show it through action.

Maybe you've left an impression that was not in alignment with the actions of godly and righteous people. That's okay! We are not perfect; nor are we expected to be. You can begin again! The first impression need not be the lasting impression. Proclaim today that you will be a vessel of light and love for those you encounter.

Proclaim today that, as you move throughout your day, you will share the beauty of God's love through your words and actions. Proclaim today that you are a beautiful child of God and are excited to live in His soft, eternal glow. Seek to leave a lasting impression that you are blessed and operate in the love, peace, mercy, and light of God.

Dear God, thank you for your many blessings. I ask today that you guide me toward making positive impressions on those I meet, and allow me to be a vessel of love, peace, mercy, and light. In Jesus' holy name, amen.

F.I.T. Step

Have you made an impression on someone you wish you could reverse? Speak to that person today. Reach out, apologize, make amends, and offer your heart to them. Restoring relationships and clearing the air is a major step towards living the life God wants you to live.

DAY 22

Choosing Healthy Fats

Eating fat will make you fat! A fat-free diet is the only way to lose weight! Tons of myths exist about fat, and many keep us from experiencing the beneficial qualities of good-for-you fats. Not all fats are bad and not all fats are created alike. In fact, some fats are actually good for you when incorporated into a healthy diet. I like to classify fat into two categories: bad fats and good fats. Let's take a moment to examine the bad fats first.

Saturated Fat is a bad fat found in beef and pork, high fat dairy, and lard. It is animal-based and can raise blood cholesterol and LDL (low-density lipoprotein level), which can increase chances for heart disease and type 2 diabetes.

Trans Fats are found primarily in vegetable oils and the foods prepared with them such as fried foods (doughnuts, French fries, deep fried fast foods), margarine and vegetable oil, baked goods (pastries, cakes), and processed snack foods (i.e., microwave popcorn). These are the most dangerous fats, as these not only raise cholesterol and LDLs but they also suppress HDLs (high density lipoprotein), which are the good cholesterol, thereby significantly increasing your chances for heart disease.

With the bad fats out of the way, we can concentrate on the good fats. The following fats have been scientifically proven to have positive health benefits when incorporated in moderation into a healthy nutritional program and active lifestyle. Many of these options can be substituted for unhealthy fats and can provide a wide range of flavor and variety!

Monounsaturated Fat can improve good cholesterol levels and help decrease risk of cardiovascular disease. Try nuts (almonds, cashews, pecans), vegetable oils (olive, canola), nut butters, and avocado.

Polyunsaturated Fat, specifically Omega-3 fatty acid, can be found in a variety of fish and fish oil such as salmon, herring, and trout, as well as in plant-based foods like tofu, walnuts, soybean oil, sunflower oil, and corn oil. These fats have been shown to decrease coronary artery disease, lower blood pressure, and even guard against irregular heartbeat.

Incorporating good fats into your diet not only can keep you healthy, but it can also improve your health in some instances. Try replacing the bad fats or oils with a healthier alternative. Not only will you still retain some of the great flavor and variety you're craving, but you'll also be doing your body good by reducing the artery-clogging bad fats and oils from your diet.

Heavenly Father, thank you for continually guiding me on my journey. Please grant me the knowledge to make the right choices when it comes to selecting healthier options. In Jesus' holy name, amen.

F.I.T. Step

Check the labels of some of your family's favorite foods. Look to see if they have trans-fats or saturated fats listed on the ingredients. If so, make the healthy choice to purchase other items that do not contain those ingredients. Incorporate healthy fats like avocados and cook with coconut and olive oil when the occasion calls for it.

DAY 23

The Tenacity of a Two-Year-Old

Blessed is the man who remains steadfast under trial, for when he has stood the test he will receive the crown of life, which God has promised to those who love him.
James 1:12, ESV

I love my third born. He was a happy surprise baby whose face strongly resembles my beloved late grandmother. He also resembles her in his nature. He is quite tenacious! He sees what he wants and will not quit until he gets it. Unlike my middle child, who dissolves into tears when he can't make his way, my two-year-old is a problem solver. If he wants something high up on a shelf, he finds something to climb on to get to it. If he can't open a door, he goes to our utility drawer, finds a screwdriver and attempts to remove the door handle. He can put on his own shoes, jacket, and hat and has recently figured out how to get in and out of his seat belt in the car.

Those are not amazing feats; many two-year-olds can do them. It is not the actions that amaze and inspire me, but rather the determination, persistence, and tenacity with which he works toward achieving his goals and desires regardless of what obstacle may stand in his way.

My two-year-old lives his life steadfastly under trial. No matter how many times he is told no, he continues to ask and work toward receiving what he desires. He is so consistent in his effort, not only is he rewarded with his wishes but sometimes his cup overflows! Tenacity is essential for accomplishment in anything you do. Without drive, determination and a strong-willed attitude, one's level of success at many endeavors will be limited in scope.

Even successful business people will agree that their achievements have been made possible due in part to their tenacity. The same goes for living a healthy, active life, and the same should also be said about living a life for Christ. You will encounter naysayers. You will come across those who do not love and support your decision to live a healthier life for Christ. Those people may try to tear you down, and if you are not steadfast in your belief, you become vulnerable to succumbing to their negativity. Be like my two-year-old. Have the willpower to never back down. Look to God for your strength, for He has promised riches far beyond your wildest dreams, but only to those who have the faith and tenacity to believe in Him regardless of their circumstances.

Dear God, thank you for life! Please encourage me to live tenaciously for you so that I may fearlessly do what you have called me here to do. In Jesus' holy name, amen.

F.I.T. Step

Make today count by being relentless in your pursuit of the things that are pleasing to Christ. Do not back down, do not doubt, listen for God, and tenaciously follow suit.

DAY 24

Motivation and Accountability

Many of my clients come to me looking for motivation. You possibly picked up this book looking for motivation as well. I hate to break it to you—you may not find it here.

Motivation is intrinsic. It comes only from within and only when you are open and ready for it. When you are ready, when you are truly inspired, genuinely open to making a change, you will inherently discover your motivation. It's deep inside, and it is our amazing God who put it there! Search within and you will find it. God wants you to find it!

While motivation comes only from within, accountability and support can come from a trusted friend, family member, or co-worker. Statistics have shown that people who have accountability partners or groups perform significantly better than those who do not. Were you ever a member of a study group in school? Did it help you perform better on tests? Likely, it did! An accountability group or accountability partner on your healthy active lifestyle journey is somewhat like a study buddy. You help one another achieve levels of success that may not have been met on your own. You encourage one another to show up on time and give your best. Sometimes you tell the honest truth (even when it may sting a bit) to support your partner or group mates in reaching their goals, and you celebrate together when milestones are accomplished!

On this journey, finding someone with whom you can partner in a mutually supportive relationship is an incredible asset that will enable you to take your results to the next level. I implore you, if you haven't already, to seek support from a friend, family member, co-worker, or even a paid professional (such as a health coach, life coach, personal trainer, or instructor) to help hold you accountable throughout this journey. With God and a compassionate accountability partner on your side, there is nothing you cannot achieve!

Heavenly Father, thank you for always being by my side. I realize I am in need of additional assistance from an understanding friend. Please direct me in the path of an accountability partner with whom I can share this journey. In Jesus' holy name, amen.

F.I.T. Step

Think about friends or family members who have some of the same goals or interests as you. Reach out to them and ask if they would like to join you on this journey. You never know, maybe they are looking for someone too!

DAY 25

Pay It Forward

Therefore, whatever you want men to do to you, do also to them, for this is the Law and the Prophets.
Matthew 7:12

In 2000, an incredible film was released. It centered on a young boy who began a school project to encourage others to pay it forward. The boy insisted that when a good deed was done, it was necessary to pay that good deed forward to the next person, that person on to the next, and so on. We see various forms of that today such as a RAK (Random Act of Kindness) Day or lines of folks paying for the coffee of the next customer in line. Anyone can pay it forward! As Christians, we are compelled to do so as an act of God's love.

On this journey, you too have the opportunity to pay it forward. So far you have learned so much. You now know the tenants of healthy eating, the benefits of exercise, and most importantly, the beauty of God's love. Your body is likely changing. Has anyone noticed? Has anyone commented lately on how bubbly and energetic you are? Is God's internal light shining through you and onto others? If so, your perseverance and dedication to this program are paying off. Congratulations! Now, the work begins.

The next time someone comments on the positive changes

he or she sees in you, thank the person and invite him or her to do the same. You can recommend this program, offer words of advice and encouragement, or even suggest getting together to fellowship. People are watching you and are influenced by the things you do. What you do matters, and you have a fantastic opportunity to pay it forward. Who knows, you may change someone else's life for the better simply by sharing your journey!

Do not be discouraged if those whom you approach are not open to your offer. Sometimes a "no" is really a "not right now." Remain available to them if you can. Leave an open invitation (you might offer a phone number or connect via social media), place those people in your prayers, continue on your journey, and perhaps in time they may decide to seek your kindness and counsel.

As a champion for Christ and a healthy living ambassador, you too can pay it forward. You need not be perfect; you need not be finished. Just be open, honest, and ready to share with an attitude of gratitude, and you too can be a blessing in someone's life.

Dearest Father, thank you for accepting me today. I pray that I have the opportunity and resiliency to reap what I sow. I desire to spread Your Word and encourage others today. In Jesus' holy name, amen.

F.I.T. Step

Approach someone today and offer a word of encouragement. Allow the conversation that ensues to flow naturally. Give the gift of kindness through word or action by paying forward the amazing gifts God has blessed you with.

DAY 26

You Can't Out-Train a Bad Diet

As a young person, I was an athlete. I was physically fit and strong. I could run fast, play sports, and was often chosen for teams. In college, I took many group fitness classes and eventually even began teaching them. I was never overweight, but it seemed no matter how much I worked out my body never changed much. I maintained a shapely figure, but I never actually looked as fit as I felt.

It was not until I began making significant changes to my nutrition that I saw the changes in my physique that I desired. I saw a drop in body fat percentage. I began to see the abs I had always envisioned. I had a more defined waistline, and my clothing sizes dropped. It wasn't until I began putting meaningful thought into what I was eating that I finally started seeing the results I desired.

I am a steadfast supporter of the 80/20/100 Rule: weight loss is most easily achieved through 80 percent nutrition, 20 percent fitness, and 100 percent mind-set. Without a proper nutrition program, the effort given in the gym will not be realized. You cannot out-train a bad diet. If you're spending hours in the gym, only to grab an unhealthy snack on the way home or reward your hard work with a favorite comfort food, you are unlikely to see the results you want. It is a careful balancing act we get to perfect over time.

I have had plenty of clients who have lost significant amounts of weight without ever once stepping foot into a gym. They've made a commitment to change by preparing their meals, skipping fast food, and saying no to sugary and alcoholic beverages—and they have seen amazing weight loss results. Once they were able to lose some weight, some chose to incorporate exercise. The weight loss gave them newfound energy and mobility, and they added the 20 percent fitness as the icing on the cake to improve their results.

Many other clients have been able to maintain their weight simply by adhering to the 80/20/100 Rule, limiting their indulgences and staying focused on the long-term goal of living a healthier, more active lifestyle. The most successful clients learn that a healthy balance enables them to live a lifestyle that is happy and manageable.

Try incorporating the 80/20/100 Rule into your lifestyle. Spend a significant amount of time planning and preparing your meals in advance, spend a bit of time getting physically active, and most importantly seek God, set your goals, and persevere through to the end!

Most gracious God, thank you for the wisdom to make good choices. Please enable me to resist temptation and follow a carefully laid out nutrition plan so I may be my healthiest self. In Jesus' holy name, amen.

F.I.T. Step

Make the decision to commit to the 80/20/100 Rule by creating a healthy menu for yourself today. Stick to your pre-planned meals and snacks and resist the urge to fall off track. Begin creating healthy habits today!

DAY 27

Refill Your Cup and It Will Overflow

Therefore their people turn to them and drink up waters in abundance.
Psalm 73:10, NIV

But seek first the kingdom of God and his righteousness, and all these things will be added to you.
Matthew 6:33

The best part of waking up…" You may recall that little ditty from the famous Folger's coffee commercials. They always depicted a healthy looking man or woman quietly waking up to the heaven-sent aromas of delicious, energizing, hot coffee. The actor poured the liquid gold into an awaiting cup, inhaled deeply, and took that first tantalizing sip. *Ahhhh.* If you recall, they never poured just a sip; it was always a full, rich cup. That full cup signified the perfect beginning to a beautiful day ahead.

The full cup of coffee is a metaphor. It reminds us that in order to be successful at serving others, we must take the time to fill our emotional, physical, and spiritual cup before we can pour into others. From the moment we awaken, we are pulled in numerous directions. Whether it's to get to a job, get kids off to school, help an elderly relative, or protest the latest social injustice, people and places depend on us to show up and complete a task efficiently. It is so easy to get caught up in the busy routine of life that we forget about ourselves. Often, it is only after we experience a personal health crisis or a setback when we realize that maybe we need to take pause to fill our own cup.

Have you filled your cup lately? Intentional prayer, healthy eating, and moderate exercise are three great ways to refill. You can take the time to live in God's presence; He will fill you more abundantly than you can imagine! You can enjoy meaningful conversation while preparing a healthy meal with a loved one. You can venture out into nature for a gratitude hike or take a group exercise class to meet some like-minded fitness enthusiasts. Whatever you choose, be sure you are filling your cup on a regular basis. God wants you to be whole and healthy. You are charged with caring for His vessel while here on earth, so treat it like fine china and be sure to keep yourself fed spiritually, nutritionally, and physically by intentionally and regularly refilling your cup—and it too shall overflow.

Creator in heaven, thank you for continued grace and mercy. I pray that you will continue to fill me with your anointed blessings. I pray to be filled with you, God. In Jesus' holy name, amen.

F.I.T. Step

Take some time for yourself today. Eat your lunch under a quiet tree or spend the afternoon at a nail salon or even read a book under the covers before bedtime. Whatever you choose, be sure to choose something that brings you joy, peace, and fulfillment.

DAY 28

Must Have At-Home Fitness Equipment

As a stay-at-home mother of three young children, it's easy to make the excuse that I simply can't get to the gym. Since I know getting to the local gym is difficult at times, and I don't want to make excuses not to exercise, I have purchased a few at-home essentials that can be useful for anyone who prefers to exercise at home for convenience or comfort. Here's to having a no-excuses mind-set:

- **Yoga or Exercise Mat** – Ideal for stretching, crunches, sit-ups, or other floor-based activities.
- **Resistance or Exercise Band Kit** – Typically comes in a variety of strengths and allows for the development of various muscle groups using resistance training techniques.
- **Exercise Ball** (large and small) – Useful for a variety of exercises from abdominals to upper and lower body and balancing tasks.
- **Fitness Loop** – Another goodie to add to strength and resistance training activities.
- **Music** – I love to listen to uplifting praise and worship music. There is a slew of free Internet radio stations that you can customize to your liking and musical options run the gamut from Gospel House to Christian

Rock, Top 100 Hits to Oldies. Find your favorites and get moving!

- **Adjustable Dumbbells** – These can be pricey; however, depending on the amount of training you do at home, these may be a worthwhile investment. They take up little space, allow for smooth transitions between heavy and lightweight activities, and are great if you're sharing the weights with a spouse or family member.
- **Treadmill/Bike/Elliptical** – Again, another extra only recommended if you are a frequent home exerciser. High-quality cardio equipment can be quite costly and is only worth the investment if you are committed to using it at least four times per week. Remember, you don't need to purchase an $800+ clothing hanger; the ones in your closet work just fine!

As a last note, many fitness DVDs exist to help you keep active while at home. And now even Internet streaming subscriptions, free YouTube videos, and Pinterest can provide many at-home workout routines to keep you on your toes. Be sure to consult a physician before starting any new fitness routine.

Heavenly Father, thank you for a healthy body. I am excited to explore new fitness options in my home, and I pray that you will guide me toward the right equipment and provide me with the motivation to complete the activities. In Jesus' holy name, amen.

F.I.T. Step

If getting to the gym has been a struggle for you, maybe working out at home is the better option. Carve out time in your day, whether it be waking up early or staying up a little later to fit in thirty minutes or more of fitness at home. Determine where you can do your workout and what equipment, music, DVDs, or other materials you will need to be successful and consistent.

DAY 29
Encourage Yourself

I keep my eyes always on the LORD. With him at my right hand, I will not be shaken.
Psalm 16:8, NIV

One of my favorite songs is "Encourage Yourself" by Donald Lawrence and the Tri-City Singers. The lyrics go as follows:

Sometimes you have to encourage yourself.
Sometimes you have to speak victory during the test.
And no matter how you feel,
speak the word and you will be healed.
Speak over yourself, encourage yourself in the Lord.

Sometimes you have to speak the word over yourself,
the pressure is all around, but God is present help.
The enemy created walls, but remember giants, they do fall;
Speak over yourself, encourage yourself in the Lord.

Something I have learned is that you will more likely encounter haters than you will encouragers. You cannot always look to others to support or encourage you on a new journey. Be still and know that God is always on your side. He is always there to support and help you. As you move forward on this journey, you will have to learn to encourage yourself. Speak victory over your journey and your progress. Here's a great verse to quote and memorize: "I can do all things through Christ who strengthens me" (Philippians 4:13).

Speak positivity to yourself daily and repeatedly. You can manifest positivity into your life simply by speaking it and believing it. When you're able to speak and see what you want for yourself, you will be able to make the things you seek a reality! Say to yourself, "I can do this; I am capable. With God I can do all things." Say it every day. Write it on a piece of paper and tape it to your mirror. Repeat it over and over again until you believe it. Let it become your happy place.

Let God's encouragement be your light in the dark, your calm in the storm, because through God you can do all things. Speak a word over yourself. Encourage yourself!

Dear Lord, thank you for waking me up this morning. I know that through you I can do all things. Please continue to strengthen and encourage me as I encourage myself in you. Please fill me with your energizing power. In Jesus' holy name, amen.

F.I.T. Step

You may find yourself at times doubtful as you go through the day. Encourage yourself with a quick "breath" prayer such as "I'm encouraged," "You strengthen me," "Fill me up," or "I can and I will." Keep these small reminders handy for times when you feel tested, and use them as ways to help you stay encouraged.

DAY 30

Restaurant Radar

When you're on a journey to lose weight or get into better health, restaurant eating is tricky. All too often, the delicious meal you get from your favorite restaurant is laden with salts, sugars, fats, and chemicals that your homemade meal would not contain. That's also why it usually tastes so good!

Understanding that avoiding restaurants altogether is close to impossible, so here are a few suggestions you can take with you to any restaurant you choose.

- Peruse the menu before visiting the restaurant. Many restaurants offer their menu online. Make some tentative selections before getting consumed by the delicious smells and impending hunger pangs.
- Select a restaurant that has a fresh salad bar or uses a fresh ingredients assembly line to create salads, sandwiches, and wraps such as a deli, fresh Mexican-American cuisine, or sub sandwich shop. This allows you to choose the ingredients and how much of each item is used.
- Look for options labeled "fit fare," "on the light side," or "under XYZ calories." These options are often accompanied by the nutrition facts and are cooked with reduced fat, sodium, and calories.
- Pass the bread or chips. You can save many calories simply by saying no.

- Choose a fresh green salad as a starter instead of soup. Pair it with a low-fat or fat-free dressing on the side so you can manage the portion size.
- Choose to drink water instead of sugary soda or cocktails. Add a lemon wedge for fun and flavor.
- Look for baked, broiled, grilled, poached, blackened, and steamed items. Those are typically healthier than their fried or sautéed counterparts.
- Ask for menu customizations; many restaurants will accommodate you. Special requests can include steaming veggies, putting dressings and sauces on the side, preparing rice without seasoning.
- Ask for an additional clean plate. When your meal arrives, divvy it up into two portions. One you will eat at the restaurant and the second can be taken by the waitperson and immediately boxed "to-go" for tomorrow's lunch. You can even share with a friend at the table, which saves fat, calories, and money!
- Share (or skip) dessert. Desserts are often designed for two or more people, so save a significant amount of fat, calories, and sugar by sharing or skipping dessert or ordering fresh fruit to satisfy that sweet tooth.

Heavenly Father, thank you for the resources to choose. Please help me resist the temptation of unhealthy meals and guide me toward meals that are good for me and my health. In Jesus' holy name, amen.

F.I.T. Step

Do some research on healthy restaurant options in your area. Choose restaurants with menus that contain healthy choices or allow customizations of the menu. The next time you and your family plan to eat out, recommend one of the places you've found and choose a great, nourishing meal.

DAY 31

Part of a Bigger Plan

For I know the thoughts that I think toward you, says the Lord, thoughts of peace and not of evil, to give you a future and a hope.
Jeremiah 29:11

When I started on my healthy, active, God-centered lifestyle journey, an amazing thing happened. I changed. From the inside out I had renewed energy, uplifted spirits, and (happily) a trimmer waistline. Much to my surprise, but just as God intended, people noticed and were inspired! They saw my newfound confidence, my increased energy level, and the bright light of God simply radiating from within me—and they wanted some too. So I shared.

I shared and shared until sharing became a passion. Friends and family were discovering the joy that loving God brings, as well as a new way to get healthy and active. After hearing God's voice encouraging me to leave my full-time career to stay home and be a more present parent, God spoke to me again. He told me that what I was doing for others was good, but that I could do more. I could inspire more people; I not only could help people become physically fit but also with His guidance, I could inspire them to become faithfully fit. Thus, this little book right here was born!

My small desire to drop a few pounds and look better in my work outfits was all part of a bigger plan God had for my life.

God has a plan for you too. He has the blueprints right there at His fingertips. While we can't easily remove those plans from our bookshelf and take a glance when convenient, we can tap into some of those plans simply by being still and connecting with God. When you ask God to speak with you, He will! Indeed, He is there waiting, ready, and excited to talk with you and guide you through His bigger plans for your life.

Perhaps this journey to better health and wellness will serve as a springboard for you to motivate, encourage, and inspire others with your story. I simply started with my friends and family! Perhaps this journey is to put into motion something incredible that you never would have been able to do if increased mobility, enhanced energy, and years added to your life were not granted to you through the benefits of better health.

What is God's plan for you? You only have to ask Him and He will guide you!

Lord God, thank you for my clear mind. I am open and receive your direction. Please guide me to do your work and your will. In Jesus' holy name, amen.

F.I.T. Step

Today, take a moment and simply be still. Raise your hands to the sky and tell God that you are ready and open. Ask Him to speak to you, to guide you. Be an open vessel and walk on the path He shows you.

DAY 32

Blender Blunders

I admit it—I'm a shake-aholic! I have a breakfast shake every morning. I absolutely love the convenience it provides me while caring for a busy family, and I also know I'm getting a healthy meal. If you're an on-the-go type person who often has to skip breakfast, I recommend you look into having a breakfast shake or smoothie to get the vitamins, minerals, and energy you need to power through your morning.

An important note, not all breakfast smoothies and shakes are made alike. It's important to know the difference between a "good" smoothie or shake and a "bad" one. Here are some easy dos and don'ts when preparing a shake or smoothie as a meal replacement:

- Do use fresh fruits or frozen fruits without added sugars or syrups.
- Do use water, unsweetened soy milk or skim (fat-free) milk as a base for your shake/smoothie.
- Do use a high protein, low fat, moderate carbohydrate protein powder or meal replacement powder.
- Do add a handful of green leafy veggies like baby kale or spinach to boost the vitamin and fiber content.
- Do use psyllium husk to add a fiber-packed punch.

- Don't use juice as a base for your shake or smoothie (use water).
- Don't use more than one half to three quarters cup of fruit per smoothie or shake.
- Don't add sugar or honey. Instead, opt for a calorie-free, natural sweetener such as stevia.
- Don't use more than one tablespoon of natural nut butter if you are aiming for weight loss results.
- Don't use large quantities of nut butters, seeds, or nuts in your smoothie.

Shakes, smoothies, and even freshly squeezed juices can be a great addition to a healthy nutrition program. Not only are they quick, easy, and convenient, but they can also offer many health benefits by providing antioxidants and micronutrients found in a wide variety of fresh, whole, natural foods. Whether you're blending a meal replacement shake created by a reputable nutrition company or creating your own meal replacement using store-bought or home-grown whole foods, following some of the above dos and don'ts will help you ensure that you're getting the most nutritional bang for your buck.

Dear Father God, thank you for waking me up today. Please bless my hands as I prepare health-conscious meals for myself and my family as I look to improve myself for your glory. In Jesus' holy name, amen.

F.I.T. Step

Purchase items from the dos list and prepare a healthy breakfast smoothie. Enjoy the benefits of whole foods and the convenience of an on-the-go shake to jump-start your day!

DAY 33

Without a Test, There Is No Testimony

My brethren, count it all joy when you fall into various trials, knowing that the testing of your faith produces patience. But let patience have its perfect work, that you may be perfect and complete, lacking nothing.
James 1:2-4

Evangelist Sandra Robinson said it best when she stated that without a test, there is no testimony.[1] Likely at some point during this journey your willpower has been tested. You may have faced a family dinner where you were tempted to eat dessert. Or perhaps a slight injury or work-related complication derailed your exercise plans. Maybe you've even questioned whether this journey is for you and whether or not you're strong enough to finish. Whatever it may be, each test simply adds to the story—the testimony—of your greatest success.

The path to greatness is lined with bumps and sharp turns. But did you know that God often uses those obstacles that get in your way as a means to assess your resilience, increase your faith, and give you something to praise Him for?

Sure, we would all love to wake up one morning at our ideal weight or perfect clothing size, blessedly stress-free and living a life of abundance and grace while at the peak of health. Who wouldn't? But what would waking up with these things simply there teach us about ourselves? During these past few weeks, you have likely learned about your weaknesses, but more importantly you've learned about your strengths. Learning about you and learning to love you, the way God intended you to be, is priceless! Each step on this journey is preparing you not just for this earthly life but for life eternal.

My own weight loss journey has been far from linear. I've had my share of ups and downs. Family vacations, injuries, lack of motivation, excuses, doubts, and distractions have all crept in and out in their own time. All praise to God, each and every time He has provided me with the means to reset, refocus, and recommit. It is not always easy. In fact, it's downright hard sometimes. As with most experiences, however, the best things come out of struggle, and with perseverance we reap the benefits.

Be joyful through your struggle and know that strength, courage, and dignity come from overcoming trial and hardship. Add these tests to your testimony. Let them be proof that you have made your way against the odds and delight in the love of the Lord, who has brought you powerfully through thus far.

Loving Father, thank you for my journey. I thank you for the tests you have assigned for me to overcome. I am gratefully humbled by your restorative power. In Jesus' holy name, amen.

F.I.T. Step

Create a list of some of the trials you have encountered on this journey. Create a list that outlines what you did to overcome those obstacles. Write a mini-praise report about the goodness of God and how He has brought you a mighty long way so far.

DAY 34

Fasting

The book of Matthew describes fasting as an important exercise for gaining clarity and becoming closer in your relationship with God. I agree! At the same time, the more extreme fasting of days past when neither food nor water was consumed for a majority of the day can be devastating to your body's internal functions.

When my clients engage in fasting, I typically make the following recommendations to them. Some of these suggestions may help you during a self-imposed or church-wide time of fasting.

Be flexible. In today's modern society, fasting can take many forms. Essentially, you are aiming to go without something you enjoy or have a tendency to overindulge in. Fasting or abstaining from specific foods or substances such as desserts, soda pop, smoking, alcohol, or even television and social media can sometimes be equally effective regarding the act of submission and discipline. The goal of fasting is to resist and replace your carnal desires for more time spent with God in prayer.

Be smart. If you are fasting from food and beverage for any significant portion of the day, be sure to keep your physical activity to a minimum, avoid prolonged sun exposure, and monitor for the side effects of dehydration and malnourishment. Signs of these can include dizziness, lightheadedness, headache, body aches, or numbness, lack of energy and focus, sleepiness, dry mouth, delayed response time, and reduction in hand-eye coordination. If you are experiencing any of these symptoms, be sure to take appropriate measures to correct them immediately.

Be realistic. Know that if you are fasting from many food groups, it is likely you will lose weight. When you strip yourself of sodium, preservatives, sugars, fats, etc., the body will respond accordingly. At the conclusion of the fast, when you begin to reincorporate those restricted food groups, you may see the weight creep back up. Don't be discouraged. Provided you are still eating healthy, keeping portions in control, and drinking water, you do not have to return to the pre-fast weight. I have known many folks who have used a church-wide Daniel Fast as a means to jump-start their long-term health results.

Fasting can take on many different shapes and lengths depending upon your needs or guidelines provided by your church community. Always consult with a medical doctor before engaging in any prolonged or highly restrictive fast and always monitor for changes in health that could be attributed to dehydration or malnourishment.

Heavenly Father, thank you for life. Please guide me in making the best of my situation today. Allow me the grace to make good decisions and follow your will. In Jesus' holy name, amen.

F.I.T. Step

Brainstorm ways you can fast effectively. If your church is calling for a fast, research the way in which you can participate that is both an honor to God, as well as safe for your body and health.

DAY 35

You Matter

Finally, brethren, whatever things are true, whatever things are noble, whatever things are just, whatever things are pure, whatever things are lovely, whatever things are of good report, if there is any virtue and if there is anything praiseworthy—meditate on these things.
Philippians 4:8

You matter and so do the choices you make. Every moment is an opportunity to move closer to God. Challenges will confront us, and the enemy will try to distract and divert us. He may come in the form of a disappointment from a friend or the illness of a relative. He may strike you on your job or in your relationship. Shucks, he may even come on a cold morning in the form of the snooze button. But remember always, you have a choice!

You can choose to stand tall against those things preventing you from walking in your greatness. God has chosen for you to be great, powerful, and steadfast. Now choose that for yourself! Others can hold you accountable and encourage you, but only you can choose to allow God to do His work in your life. He will show you the path, but you must choose to put one foot in front of the other.

Examine some of the choices you've made over the past

few days. Were they choices that align with God's perfect will? Were they choices that brought you closer to God by serving Him? Today I encourage you to make choices that are pleasing to God—choices that bring you closer to Him, choices that renew your mind, body, and spirit. Remember that your body is a vessel through which God shows His love, and it is up to you to maintain it! Make healthy choices today that enable you to use the gifts you've been entrusted with in powerful and meaningful ways for many days to come.

You matter. You are important. You are an integral part of God's plan, and He is intentional. The choices you make today will influence the places and spaces you visit and those whom you encounter. God put you on Earth to make it better simply by being present!

You are wanted, needed, and loved. God loves you with an undying affection that transcends this world. He is glorified and you are strengthened when the choices you make magnify and uplift Him and His Word. Never forget that you matter to this world, and you matter to God.

Most gracious God, thank you for caring for me. Today, I place you at the center of my life. You are the captain of this ship, and I am your trusting passenger. Please guide me on this path because what I do matters on Earth and in eternity. In Jesus' holy name, amen.

F.I.T. Step

Look in the mirror today and tell yourself, "I matter." It is important that you understand how integral you are in the fabric of this world. Encourage someone by letting that person know how much he or she matters to you, as well as to God.

DAY 36

Living Healthy as a Family

Beginning a new lifestyle can be difficult, and doing so without family support can be even more challenging. Getting a spouse, a partner, or even kids to team up with you in eating healthy, getting active, and honoring God in more meaningful ways is a job in itself. While you may be ready for a sweeping overhaul, others around you may not. Making small changes over time can encourage your household to be healthy together.

You may be met with a few raised eyebrows or disappointed looks when your teenager goes to the pantry looking for his favorite after-school snack and is faced with something healthy. It's okay! Change takes time. Be encouraged that you are doing what is best for those around you. Most importantly, hold steadfast in your own journey. Do not let a family member who does not support your journey to a healthier, happier you derail your ambition. Remember, God wants what is best for you, and though you might encounter roadblocks in the most unlikely of places, you are on the right track and can power through!

Here are some great family-friendly ideas for promoting a healthy, active lifestyle:

- Grocery shop and prepare meals together.
- Institute family walks after large meals.

- Trade in Friday Pizza and Movie night for a family night out doing something active like bowling, roller skating, or miniature golf.
- Buy fun lunch boxes and write one another notes to place in the boxes as you prepare lunches together each day.
- Join a community center that offers activities for the whole family (e.g., a kids' program, classes, gym equipment, recreation club, etc.).
- Encourage friendly competition (e.g., who can drink the most water in a day, who gets active five or more times a week, who passes on desserts and unhealthy snacks for a full week, etc.) and award non-food prizes like a gift card for a DVD or video game, a "chore-free day" coupon, or tickets to a favorite event or activity.

Getting healthy and growing together spiritually as a family can be life changing. It can bring the family unit closer together and promote a sense of unity and love. When possible, include your family in your journey and allow them to reap the benefits of living life abundantly.

Dear God, thank you for my beautiful life. Please help me to be an encouragement to my family. I pray that I can be an inspiration to them to make changes that will bring us all closer to you and closer to one another.

F.I.T. Step

Choose a few small steps that you can take over the next few days to encourage healthy, active, prayerful living amongst your household. Plan a family night that incorporates a healthy meal, a fun activity, and ends with a meaningful prayer of thanksgiving.

DAY 37

Quality vs. Quantity

This is the confidence we have in approaching God: that if we ask anything according to his will, he hears us.
1 John 5:14, NIV

If you're up to speed on social media, you may have seen those comedic video renditions of the relative that prays too long over the Thanksgiving dinner. It's typically an older relative who thanks the Good Lord Jesus the Christ for everything (and anything) under the sun. From the turkey to the end of violence to the neighbor's smelly cat, the prayer goes on and on as everyone around the table makes sideways glances, checks their watches, or even falls asleep. Sometimes these prayers are so lengthy, even the lemon meringue pie's whipped plumes begin to deflate!

Lengthy prayers can be intimidating, especially to new believers. Seasoned Christians often speak powerful words that address the needs of everyone gathered and elicit audible agreements from the crowd. New Christians may be led to ask themselves, "Are their prayers better than mine? Does God like longer, more verbose prayer? If these people are the leaders and elders of my church, then they must be doing it right, right?" Take heart and be reminded that God hears all prayers, whether they're graceful and protracted or short and choppy.

God hears you when you say a breath prayer asking Him for favor as you're walking down the street. And He hears you when you thank Him for bringing you through a difficult situation or for gracing you with a new gift or opportunity. He even hears you when you express your anger, disappointment, and frustration. Talk to God like you would talk to your best friend. God really is your best friend, you know! He knows you better than anyone. So, no need to put on the false pretenses!

Most importantly, God wants to hear from us. He wants us to serve Him. He is not as concerned with how long our prayer is; He is interested in the quality of our prayer and our sincerity in living His Word and acting upon His faith. God wants quality not quantity. It is pleasing to God if you're able to spend many moments in prayer but if you're simply going through the motions, it is for naught.

Give God quality time, quality love, and quality prayer, and He will be pleased with your faithfulness and cover you with His grace.

Father God, thank you for amazing grace. You know my heart, and you know my ways. Please help me to choose You over all else. I want less of me and more of you in a meaningful way. In Jesus' holy name, amen.

F.I.T. Step

Spend your day living a life of quality. Give God quality time. Listen to your children, partner, or friends with intentionality. It matters not if you complete a million tasks if they are not done correctly and carefully. Focus on the things that matter by giving them the quality attention they deserve.

DAY 38

Don't Be Saddled by the Scale

Weight loss is not linear. It is not a comfortable, steady roll down a hill. It is not a car that can accelerate from zero to sixty in a matter of moments. Weight loss is bumpy, curvy, twisty, and turny. Some weeks you will see a lot of progress on the scale while other weeks you may see nothing. There may even be weeks where you see those numbers creep up! That is normal.

The body fluctuates significantly based on a great number of factors. Water retention, hormones, stress, rest (or lack thereof), and muscle gain can all influence the number on the scale. You can be doing everything right—following your meal plan, counting calories, drinking water, exercising—yet still see no scale results. Do not get discouraged. Begin to look at the numerous other ways you are changing and celebrate those non-scale victories. Some great non-scale victories that can be tracked include:

- Inches lost. Taking regularly scheduled, accurate measurements can be a great indicator of fat loss.
- Clothing getting looser, belt notches moving or new (smaller) clothing sizes being purchased.
- Increased endurance. This can be indicated by faster walking or jogging speeds and/or the ability to accomplish difficult physical activities with increased ease.

- Passing up favorite go-to comfort foods in exchange for healthier alternatives.
- Advancement in discipline and commitment to a program.
- Increase in moments of happiness, increase in energy, improved focus and mental stamina.
- Improvement in medical test results such as cholesterol, blood pressure, and blood sugar levels.
- Clearer skin, brighter eyes, growing fingernails and hair, and an overall sense of well-being.

Since oftentimes we rate our success level based on the scale, be sure to incorporate some of these non-scale indicators of success and celebrate them just as you would pounds released on the scale. I recommend keeping a journal of victories so that you are able to document your results. Reward yourself consistently for both the scale and non-scale wins. Sometimes when we are closest to our goal is precisely when we find ourselves faced with some of the biggest obstacles. Isn't that just like the enemy? If that obstacle for you is the scale, take a moment to reflect on the above list as alternate indicators of your hard work and dedication, and ultimately, use them as helpful stepping stones on the road to long-term success!

Dear God, thank you for believing in me. As I continue on this journey, please help me look beyond the scale to the whole of my progress. I seek to please you with my efforts as each step I take I am striving to get closer to You. In Jesus' holy name, amen.

F.I.T. Step

Write down your non-scale victories. Have you been committed to your nutrition plan? Did you skip dessert last night? Have you been making good use of your gym membership or at-home DVDs? Acknowledge and celebrate these wins with a friend or family member.

DAY 39

Bringing it Full Circle

In those days I, Daniel, was mourning three full weeks. I ate no pleasant food, no meat or wine came into my mouth, nor did I anoint myself at all, till three whole weeks were fulfilled.
Daniel 10:2-3

You and Daniel now have something in common. You have both spent a multitude of days experiencing something life-changing. Daniel turned away from food and drink and you turned toward a new, healthier, happier, more God-centered lifestyle. Shout your praises to the Lord, because it is with Him by your side that you have made it through!

At the conclusion of twenty-one days, Daniel began consuming food and drink, but he did so a changed man. Now, as you come to the end of this leg of your journey, I encourage you to continue to avoid the temptation of slipping back into old habits and old mind-sets. My prayer for you is that through this process you have been renewed in mind, body, and spirit. I pray this experience has touched your life in an indelible way and that with this newfound freedom you will continue to forge forward upon the wings of God's grace and mercy.

Maurette Brown Clark reminds us in song that "It ain't over." God is not done with us. He is still working on our minds and hearts and is standing by our side as we press forward. He is our champion, provider, and faithful leader. He will cheer for you, fight for you, love you, and keep you. He loves you so much that He gave His only son for you. You will be victorious!

Take these final days to commit to yourself and God that you will live faithfully, intentionally, and tenaciously. Commit to making healthy choices, ones that are good for your mind, body, and spirit. Commit to taking care of and loving yourself. Commit to praising God and helping others. Commit to being who God says you are. Do not waver in your faith and love for Him and His great Word. God provides all of our needs according to His will for our lives, and He will continue to grace you with the power to continue the progress you've begun here during the days of this portion of your journey.

Awesome God, thank you for new experiences. I pray that you keep my heart and mind open to your Word. It is by faith that I walk towards building relationship with you. Thank you for guiding me thus far, and I pray for continued guidance as I continue to answer your call upon my life. In Jesus' holy name, amen.

F.I.T. Step

You have arrived! The time has come to reflect upon the past days during this journey. You've likely had some challenges and also some triumphs. Continue to press on. Don't let this be the end for you. You have embarked upon a wonderful, life-long, transformative journey. Pray to God today to give you guidance moving forward on this walk.

DAY 40

It's a Lifestyle, Not a Diet

Take a moment and recall all the information you've acquired during this journey. Everything you have learned and practiced are tools that can (and should) be taken with you beyond this program. You now have skills you can incorporate into your everyday life to maintain the results you've achieved so far or to continue to your final destination. This is not just a diet.

This is a lifestyle change. Hopefully, you've grown spiritually and emotionally, have developed the discipline to stick to a program, and have seen amazing health results in the process. Here are some key takeaways I hope you're able to continue to use and implement in your lifestyle journey:

- Put God first. He is the guide and anchor in your life and He will not steer you wrong.
- Maintain a consistent eating schedule and make meal preparation a priority.
- When in doubt, choose whole foods over processed items.
- Incorporate water (at least half your body weight in water ounces) daily for great health benefits.
- Find an accountability partner or group to help you stay on track and focused.

- Set aside time for yourself and take advantage of the occasional opportunity to put yourself first.
- Remember the 80/20/100 Rule: 80 percent nutrition, 20 percent fitness, 100 percent mind-set.
- Enjoy the process, seek God, and don't give up.

Congratulations for making the choice to change! You can do all things through Christ, and He will strengthen you in everything you do. Celebrate your wins and continue to reflect on the things that challenge you. Find new ways to make eating healthy, getting active, and loving God in a more meaningful way fun, new, and exciting. So many doors will open as you step into the person God has created you to be.

Father God, I thank you for this journey. I thank you for my time here on Earth, and I am excited to continue living a life filled with you and for you. I pray you continue to strengthen me as I do work for your kingdom. In Jesus' holy name, amen.

F.I.T. Step

Continue to live this healthy, active, God-centered lifestyle daily, beyond the pages of this book. You can do all things through Christ, and all things are done for His glory. Write down long-term goals for yourself and set some milestones along the way. Whether your goal is big or small, the ultimate goal is to live a healthy, active life for Christ, and you are well on your way to making a new, amazing lifestyle!

APPENDIX
The Recipes

I enjoy the freedom and flexibility that cooking at home enables me to have with regards to my health results. While you are on this journey, I encourage you to do as much cooking at home as possible. It gives you so much opportunity to control what goes into your body and can be very budget-friendly!

Each recipe in this appendix is perfect for the whole family, great for lunch or dinner, and can even be divvied up into plastic containers, refrigerated or frozen, and used as easy heat-and-eat meals throughout the week. Each recipe serves four unless otherwise noted.

MAINS

Mama's Lasagna (serves 8)
1lb lean ground turkey (original or Italian seasoned)
1 garlic clove, minced
1 box whole wheat lasagna noodles
15oz part-skim ricotta cheese
½ package frozen spinach (thawed)
2 cups low-fat mozzarella cheese
½ cup Parmesan cheese
28oz Newman's Own Marinara, Sockarooni, Bombolina or

Tomato-Based Sauce of choice. 24oz/4oz
basil, garlic powder or salt-free Italian spice blend
cooking spray

Directions:

1. Preheat oven to 350°F, boil lasagna noodles according to package directions.
2. In medium mixing bowl, combine ricotta, spinach, 1 cup mozzarella, Parmesan, basil, and garlic powder. Set aside.
3. In large skillet, heat cooking spray and sauté minced garlic. Add ground turkey and cook to an internal temperature of 165°F. Add basil or Italian seasoning per preference. Add all sauce (except for 4 oz) and simmer for 10 minutes. Set aside.
4. Spray 13x9 baking pan with cooking spray. Spread even layer of meat-free sauce at bottom of pan. Layer noodles followed by half ricotta mixture followed by half meat sauce mixture. Repeat for a second layer or noodles, ricotta, meat sauce. Cover with final layer of noodles. Top noodles with remaining meat-free sauce and sprinkle even layer of remaining mozzarella.
5. Cover with aluminum foil and bake for 45 minutes until bubbly. Remove aluminum foil and continue to bake for 10 minutes

Cajun Seasoned Catfish

4 (4-6oz) catfish fillets
1 tbsp fresh lemon juice
4 tsp sodium-free Cajun seasoning (Mrs. Dash/Bayou Rub)
cooking spray
lemon wedges

Directions:

1. Preheat broiler to 500°F, coat broiler pan with cooking spray.
2. Brush both sides of catfish with lemon juice and sprinkle with Cajun seasoning.
3. Place fish on pan and broil for 5 minutes (each side), or

until fish flakes easily with a fork.

4. Serve with lemon wedges per preference.

Grilled Tilapia Tacos

6 (6oz) tilapia fillets
1 tbsp ground chipotle seasoning
1.5 tsp ground cumin
2 tbsp olive oil
1 tsp lime zest
2 tbsp fresh lime juice
12 corn tortillas or lettuce wraps (for lower carb alternative)
1 cup shredded cole slaw mix
mango salsa (or other store-bought fruity salsa blend)
fresh lime wedges
cooking spray

Directions:

1. Combine cumin and chipotle and rub over fillets.
2. Stir olive oil, lime zest, and lime juice together and rub over fillets.
3. Spray griddle or pan with cooking spray and grill over medium-high heat 3 minutes (each side), or until fish flakes easily with a fork.
4. Cool to handle and shred fish. Place 2-3 tablespoons of fish into each tortilla topping with slaw and salsa. Add a final squeeze of lime juice before serving.

Summer Sweet Glazed Chicken

4 (5oz) boneless, skinless chicken breasts
1 cup sugar-free apricot preserves
1/3 cup orange juice
¼ cup Smart Start**
¼ tsp ground black pepper
cooking spray

Directions:

1. Preheat oven to 350°F and spray roasting pan with cooking spray.

2. Prepare glaze: Combine preserves, orange juice, and smart start.
3. Rub chicken breasts with the glaze, sprinkle pepper on top, place in roasting pan.
4. Cook for 20 minutes, basting chicken every 5 minutes with excess glaze from bottom of the pan.

Garlic-Ginger Poached Chicken Breast

4 (6oz) boneless, skinless chicken breasts
4 cups low-sodium, fat-free chicken broth
1 cup chopped carrots
1 celery stalk, sliced thinly
½ yellow onion, finely chopped
2 tbsp chopped fresh ginger
1 tbsp chopped garlic
¼ low-sodium soy sauce
½ cup trimmed snow peas
2 tbsp chopped chives

Directions:

1. In a large saucepan, bring broth to a boil.
2. Add carrots, celery, ginger, garlic, onion and soy sauce. Cover and simmer for 10 minutes.
3. Add chicken breasts and cook until broth returns to boiling. Turn chicken and simmer for 3 minutes.
4. Add snow peas and continue to cook another 3 minutes, or until chicken is just cooked.
5. Serve chicken in large, shallow serving bowls, spoon broth over chicken and garnish with chives.

Spicy Chicken and Okra

3 tbsp low-carb bake mix (Carbquick, Bob's Redmill, Atkins Quick Quisine)
¼ tsp ground black pepper
1½ pounds boneless, skinless chicken thighs (cut into 1.5-inch pieces)
2 tsp coconut or canola oil
½ can (7ozs) no-salt-added diced tomatoes

2 tbsp chopped garlic
2/3 cup low-sodium, fat-free chicken broth
½ tsp crushed red pepper
1 tsp salt-free Cajun seasoning (Mrs. Dash/Bayou Rub)
10oz frozen cut okra (thawed)

Directions:

1. Combine bake mix and black pepper in a gallon size zipper bag, add chicken and shake to coat.
2. Heat canola oil in a nonstick skillet until hot, add chicken and brown on all sides (about 5 minutes).
3. Add tomatoes, garlic, broth red pepper and Cajun seasoning, bring to a boil, cover, and simmer 10-15 minutes until chicken is cooked through.
4. Add okra, cover and simmer another 5 minutes, or until okra is soft.

Pepper Steak

2 tbsp black pepper
1 tsp dried rosemary
4 beef tenderloins (approx. 5oz each)
2 tbsp healthy margarine (like Smart Start)
2 tbsp olive oil
1 cup dry red wine

Directions:

1. Combine pepper and rosemary in large bowl and cover both sides of each tenderloin with the rub.
2. Heat margarine and olive oil in skillet until melted. Add tenderloins and cook over medium-high heat for 5-7 minutes, flipping mid-way through.
3. Remove tenderloins and transfer to plate.
4. Add wine to skillet, bring to boil over high heat until sauce reduces to half. Spoon sauce over steaks.

Fit Friday Fish Fry

1 ½ pounds grouper (cod, haddock work too) fillets
1 tbsp fat-free mayonnaise

1 tbsp fresh lime juice
1/8 tsp black pepper
1/8 tsp onion powder
½ cup fresh bread crumbs
1½ tbsp unsalted butter (or margarine like Smart Start–lowers fat/cholesterol)
cooking spray
2 tbsps chopped fresh parsley (optional)

Directions:

1. Preheat oven to 425°F.
2. Spray 11 x 7-inch baking dish with cooking spray and place fish fillets flat. Combine mayo, lime juice, pepper, onion powder in a small bowl and spread over fish. Sprinkle with bread crumbs and drizzle with butter/margarine.
3. Bake until fish is cooked through and flakes with a fork (about 20 minutes). Sprinkle with parsley and serve hot.

Baked Herb Chicken Breast

4 (6oz) boneless, skinless chicken breasts (rinsed and patted dry)
2 tbsps olive oil or coconut oil
spices and herbs of choice: garlic powder, onion powder, basil, parsley, oregano, thyme, etc.
cooking spray

Directions:

1. Preheat oven to 400°F; spray baking dish with cooking spray.
2. Cover chicken breasts in desired spices and herbs and place flat in baking dish, rub parchment paper with olive oil and place parchment, oil side down, on top of and snugly around the chicken breasts.
3. Bake until chicken reaches an internal temperature of 165°F (likely around 25-40 minutes).

Basic Baked Salmon

4 (6oz) salmon fillets

seasonings of choice (basil, pepper, garlic powder, onion powder, Mrs. Dash salt-free seasonings, etc.)
lemon wedges (optional)
cooking spray

Directions:

1. Preheat oven to 425°F, line a baking dish with aluminum foil and spray foil with cooking spray.
2. Arrange fillets flat on pan, sprinkle with seasonings of choice, squeeze of lemon juice top (optional).
3. Bake filets for 20-25 minutes, or until fish flakes easily with a fork.

One-Skillet Complete Lemon Chicken Dinner Bake

12oz baby red potatoes, washed and halved
1 tbsp olive oil divided
4 (6oz) skinless, boneless chicken breast halves, pounded to 3/4-inch thickness
3/4 tsp sea salt, divided
1/2 tsp ground black pepper, divided
2 thyme sprigs
4 oz cremini mushrooms, quartered
1 tbsp chopped fresh thyme
1/4 cup 2% milk
5 tsp all-purpose flour
1 3/4 cups fat-free, low-sodium chicken stock
8 very thin lemon slices
1 (8-ounce) package trimmed French-style green beans
2 tbsps chopped parsley

Directions:

1. Preheat oven to 450°F.
2. Place potatoes in a medium saucepan, cover with water and bring to a boil, reduce to simmer for 12 minutes or until tender, drain.
3. Heat a large ovenproof skillet over medium-high heat. Add 1 teaspoon oil to pan.
4. Sprinkle chicken with 1/4 tsp sea salt and 1/4 tsp black

pepper. Add chicken and thyme sprigs to pan; cook 5 minutes or until chicken is browned. Turn chicken over.

5. Place pan in oven and bake for 10 minutes or until chicken is done (internal temperature of 165°F. Remove chicken from pan, set aside.
6. Return pan to medium-high heat. Add remaining 2 teaspoons oil. Add potatoes, cut sides down; mushrooms; and 1 tbsp thyme; cook 3 minutes or until browned, stirring once.
7. Combine milk and flour in a small bowl, stirring with a whisk.
8. Add remaining salt, remaining pepper, flour mixture, stock, lemon, and green beans to pan; simmer 1 minute or until slightly thickened.
9. Add chicken; cover, reduce heat and simmer 3 minutes or until green beans are crisp-tender. Sprinkle with parsley.

Baked Ziti (serves 8)

1lb extra lean ground turkey
1 clove garlic, minced
1 tbsp olive oil
1lb box Barilla Pasta plus mostaccioli pasta (or short whole wheat pasta of choice)
1lb jar of Newman's Own Tomato Basil Bombolina Sauce
2 cups low-fat mozzarella cheese
basil, salt, black pepper (to taste)
cooking spray

Directions:

1. Bring 1 quart water to boil, add pasta and cook per package directions. Be sure to leave pasta *al dente,* or just a little bit firm. Preheat oven to 350°F.
2. In non-stick skillet, spray with cooking spray and lightly cook garlic, Add olive oil and ground turkey. While turkey browns, add salt, black pepper and basil to taste. Be sure to break meat apart and flip frequently to avoid burning.
3. Once turkey has reached internal temperature of 165°F, add tomato basil sauce and set to simmer about 5 minutes.

4. Combine pasta and meat sauce in casserole pan. Cover with aluminum foil and transfer to oven. Cook about 10 minutes. Uncover, top with mozzarella and return to oven to melt cheese (about 10 minutes). Serve hot.

Jerk Turkey Burgers

Jerk rub

1 tbsp each:
- onion powder
- dried onion flakes
- garlic powder
- ground ginger
- dried thyme
- light brown sugar
- ground red pepper

2 tsps each:
- ground allspice
- coarsely ground black pepper
- ground coriander

1 tsp ground cinnamon

½ tsp each:
- ground nutmeg
- ground cloves

1/3 cup freeze dried chives

Jamaican Jerk Rub: Add all ingredients in a blender or food processor and blend until ground and well blended.

Burger

1 lb lean or extra lean ground turkey
1 cup finely chopped red onion
1 tbsp Jamaican jerk rub
1 large egg white
¼ cup low-sodium sweet and sour sauce
¼ cup finely chopped red, green or yellow bell pepper

Directions:

1. Combine onion, jerk rub, egg white, sweet and sour sauce

and bell pepper and stir well. Hand mix with ground turkey, divide into four equivalent portions and shape into 1" thick round patties. Cover and refrigerate for 30 minutes.

2. Heat skillet or grill, spray each side of patty with cooking spray and grill until internal temperature of 165°F flipping mid-way through (about 8-10 minutes per side).
3. Serve on whole wheat buns, with a side of roasted vegetables or place atop crisp salad greens.

Sassy Shrimp Fajitas

1 ½ cup red, green or yellow bell pepper strips
1 small red onion, sliced lengthwise
2 tsps garlic, minced
½ cup green salsa (store bought-I love Frontera Grill brand)
1 tsp ground coriander
salt to taste
1 ½ lb large shrimp (peeled and deveined)
8 (6-inch) corn tortillas or lettuce wraps (for lower carb alternative)
2 tbsp chopped fresh cilantro
cooking spray

Directions:

1. Heat large skillet over medium-high heat, coat pan with cooking spray. Add peppers, garlic, and onion and sauté for 4 minutes. Add salsa, salt coriander, and shrimp and continue sautéing until shrimp are done (about 2-3 minutes).
2. Arrange about ½ cup of shrimp mixture at center of tortilla or lettuce wrap and sprinkle with cilantro to preference.

SIDES

Spaghetti Squash (serving varies)

1 large spaghetti squash
1 tbsp olive oil

Directions:

1. Preheat oven to 425°F. Clean squash, remove any labels. Cut squash lengthwise and scoop out seeds.
2. Fill baking pan with ½ inch water. Place squash halves face down in water. Bake for 30-40 minutes. Flip squash and continue baking 15 minutes.
3. Remove squash, allow to cool slightly and scrape inside of squash with a fork creating long strings. Toss with olive oil in large bowl.

Mashed Cauliflower

1 head cauliflower (cut into florets)
1 tbsp olive oil
1 clove garlic, smashed
¼ cup Parmesan cheese, grated
1 tbsp reduced fat cream cheese
salt and black pepper to taste

Directions:

1. Steam cauliflower in steamer insert in large pot of water until tender (about 10 minutes).
2. In skillet, heat olive oil, and garlic until softened (about 2 minutes) and remove from heat.
3. Once tender, drain and transfer half of the cauliflower to a food processor and blend. Add remaining cauliflower florets slowly until creamy. Add garlic, Parmesan, cream cheese, and salt/pepper and blend until combined. Serve immediately.

Vegetarian Greens

2 lbs of greens (collard, turnip, mustard) cleaned, chopped and rinsed

1 can no salt added diced tomatoes
1 cup low-sodium, Imagine "no chicken" broth or vegetable broth
½ yellow onion, chopped
1 tsp minced garlic
2 tbsp olive oil
red pepper flakes, garlic powder, onion powder, basil, to taste

Directions:

1. In large pot over medium heat, sauté onions in olive oil until translucent, add garlic.
2. Add half of the greens and stir to incorporate.
3. Add diced tomatoes (including liquid) and second half of greens.
4. Add broth as greens cook down, stirring occasionally and add seasonings of preference.
5. Greens should simmer for 20-30 minutes until soft.

Vegetarian Quinoa Risotto

2 tsp olive oil
1 cup chopped yellow onion
¼ cup chopped celery
1 tsp minced garlic
1 cup quinoa, rinsed well
2 cups low-sodium, fat-free chicken broth or Imagine "no chicken" broth
2 cups chopped spinach or Swiss chard
½ roughly chopped mushrooms
¼ cup grated Parmesan cheese
¼ tsp ground black pepper
pinch sea salt

Directions:

1. Heat olive oil in a saucepan and add onion and celery, tossing until soft (about 5 minutes).
2. Add quinoa and garlic and cook for one minute, stir occasionally.

3. Add broth and bring to boil, reduce heat to simmer for 12 minutes.
4. Add greens and mushrooms and cook for 2 additional minutes.
5. Remove from heat, add cheese, salt, and pepper.

Oven Roasted Asparagus

12-14 asparagus spears (ends trimmed)
1 Tbsp olive oil
¼ tsp (each) sea salt, black pepper
¼ cup shredded Parmesan or asiago cheese

Directions:

1. Preheat oven to 425°F.
2. In a shallow glass baking dish, toss asparagus spears, olive oil, salt, and pepper, arrange spears to lay flat
3. Bake 12-18 minutes until asparagus is tender; sprinkle with cheese.

Zesty Italian-Style Broccoli

1 pound fresh broccoli
1 tsp olive oil or coconut oil
1 Tbsp lemon juice
1 clove garlic, minced
pinch (each) sea salt, ground black pepper

Directions:

1. Trim, peel, and cut broccoli into florets with 2-inch stems and slice remaining stems into ½ inch slices.
2. Bring 1 quart water to a boil in large saucepan, add broccoli and garlic, return to boil, reduce heat to medium-high and cook uncovered for 3-5 minutes or until tender. Drain.
3. In separate bowl, combine oil, lemon juice, sea salt and black pepper. Pour over broccoli. Cover and let stand for 5-10 minutes to allow flavors to blend. Toss, serve.

NOTES

1. Evangelist Sandra Robinson led the Lydia's Circle monthly women's empowerment group at Christ Community Church March 26, 2016.

ABOUT THE AUTHOR

Gabriella Marigold Lindsay, M.Ed, is a wife and mother first, but given the opportunity to write and speak, she inspires many. As a health coach, nutrition educator, group fitness instructor and personal trainer, she has helped people across the world reach their health and fitness goals through in-person and online programs.

Gabriella is also actively involved in her church, Christ Community Church in South Holland, Illinois. She leads the Faithfully Fit Community Fitness Ministry, volunteers in the Children's Church Ministry and serves on the leadership team of the Women's Ministry. She believes that the mind-body-spiritual connection is essential to creating a happy and whole person.

Gabriella writes a blog at www.theslayathomemom.com, where she chronicles her journey as a mother, a devout Christian, an advocate for women's empowerment, and a proponent of health and wellness. She enjoys spending time with her husband and three young children doing kid-friendly outdoor activities. *Living F.I.T.: A 40-Day Guide to Living Faithfully, Intentionally, and Tenaciously* is her first book.

For more of Gabriella's writings:

http://theslayathomemom.com

Made in the USA
Coppell, TX
07 March 2021

51397695R00061